BORN IN SIBERIA
Tamara Astafieva

Born in Siberia is the story of a remarkable Russian
woman and her family from just after the 1917
revolution until the present, told in her own words,
together with some explanatory notes and occasional
commentary by Michael Darlow and her friend,
Luba Ioffe.

Tamara Astafieva's story, which in places reads like
one of the traditional fables from the beautiful but
fearsome land in which she was born, is also the story
of millions of other ordinary Russians and their
families during this last, most troubled century in her
vast country's long and turbulent history.

BORN IN SIBERIA
Tamara Astafieva

Edited by
MICHAEL DARLOW
AND
DEBBIE SLATER

Translations and other assistance
LUBA IOFFE

QUARTET

First published in 2014 by
Quartet Books Limited
A member of the Namara Group
27 Goodge Street, London WIT 2LD

A catalogue record for this book
is available from the British Library

ISBN 978 0 7043 7334 1

Typeset by Antony Gray
Printed and bound in Great Britain by
T J International Ltd, Padstow, Cornwall

To my friend Alexei Piterskikh,
with deep appreciation of his various God-given
talents and a wonderful sense of humour.

Arctic Ocean

East Siberian
Sea

Laplev Sea

Kolyma

(U.S.)

Bering Sea

Lena

Vilyuy

Aldan

Sea of
Okhotsk

Yenisey

S I B E R I A

Angara

Lena

Bratsk

Amur

Lake
Baikal

CHINA

Amur

Sea of
Japan

MONGOLIA

JAPAN

N. KOREA

SOVIET UNION
about 1989

S. KOREA

Yellow
Sea

East China Sea

| 0 | 400 | 800 | 1200 Kilometres |

| 0 | | 400 | 800 Miles |

Introduction

Michael Darlow

Between 1966 and 1968 I worked in Russia on two major television co-productions between the British ITV company, Granada
and the main Soviet press and information agency, APN Novosti.
During that time I worked closely with a number of Russians but
one in particular stood out, a beautiful young woman called
Tamara. Tamara was a senior editor in Novosti's television department who had been assigned by the agency to be our researcher
and chief fixer in Russia. In the bureaucratic minefield, controlled
by often deliberately obstructive petty officials, which was the
Soviet Union of the mid-1960s, this was no easy task, even for
someone who, like Tamara, was acting for an official Soviet
government organisation. During my frequent visits to Russia
during those years I got to know Tamara well. I met her young
son and her husband and learned a little about her life. Then,
towards the end of our work together, Tamara fell out of favour
with her Russian bosses and another woman, a stern-faced party
apparatchik, was assigned to take on her role during the final stages
of the production of the second film. In the spring of 1969 I made
one final visit to Moscow during which I was able to persuade
Tamara's bosses to bring Tamara to the offices of Novosti so that I
could have one final meeting with her. In order to reduce the
possibility of our conversation being overheard I invited Tamara
to go for a walk with me around Moscow. During that short
walk, through the crowded city streets, Tamara told me a little
about what had caused her official fall from grace. After that one
final, short meeting I did not see Tamara again. I did not return to
Russia for many years and, although over the years I did have very

occasional contact with two other Russians who I had worked with in the 1960s, I lost touch with Tamara completely.

Then, almost forty years later, after the fall of the Soviet regime, out of the blue my wife and I received a letter from Tamara. In it she told us something about her life since our last meeting. With the letter she sent a short book of poems which she had written and three impressionistic essays in which she described important events in her life and the lives of members of her family. A correspondence began and Tamara sent more poems, descriptions of important emotional and imaginative events in her life and a series of short pieces which she called 'hieroglyphs' – (literally, a partially pictographic, condensed form of script, especially associated with ancient Egypt, a symbol used to convey a secret, philosophical or spiritual meaning). Over time a deeply personal and moving picture started to emerge of the life of one typical, but also exceptional, Russian woman and her family from shortly after the 1917 Bolshevik Revolution until the present day. I began to suspect that here, in the life of this one woman, Tamara, and her family, was a distillation, an archetype, for the lives and experiences of millions of other ordinary Russians across the decades since 1917. Reading Tamara's work has, I believe, deepened my understanding of Russia and of the feelings and experience of Russians of my own generation, the generation that lived through the Second World War, the Cold War and the years since the collapse of the Soviet Bloc.

I told my long-time friend and publisher Naim Attallah, the proprietor of Quartet Books, about Tamara's writing and my thoughts about it and he too read Tamara's material. He came to the same conclusion as me and the result is this short book. It is made up of a selection of Tamara's writings, her essays and descriptions of her life and the things that have happened to her and her family, plus a selection of her poems. Where necessary I have inserted sections of explanatory commentary, background information and footnotes, together with some extracts from letters which I wrote home during the time while I was working with Tamara. Before most of Tamara's essays I have inserted the date or year in which the events she describes occurred so as to give readers a sense of the chronology of Tamara's life. There is also a postscript written by Tamara's friend and translator, Luba Ioffe.

Bradford on Avon
March 2013

Prologue

Tamara Astafieva

22 February 1937
Siberia – they say the word is both mysterious and
attractive – Siberia, the blessed Russian land, the land
of the descendants of Yermak the Cossack leader in
the reign of Ivan the Terrible, known for his
conquest of Siberia in 1582.

Actually, I almost came into this world right on top of our warm Russian stove. But my mother had just enough time to realise that the stove was not the best place to deliver a baby and, despite of the weight and size of her belly, somehow managed to crawl down on to the floor. My father worked close to our house, at the railway station (he was the station master) and, when he heard my mother's cries, rushed home to find my mother spread-eagled on the floor screaming like mad. Although he had no idea what he ought to do in such a situation he nevertheless immediately started trying to help her . . .

It was February. Everywhere was white: in Siberia there is no lack of snow. In the distance the three big rivers of Siberia were roaring: the Ob, the Biya, and the Katun. But in the house where somebody was being born in pain and blood no one heard them: the room was full of sounds of its own. My father delivered me and found a bit of cloth to dry me with, but he did not dare to cut the umbilical cord. So he left me connected to my mother by the cord and ran to find someone who could deal with it. He found help and at last I was washed in warm water, wrapped in clean sheets and put on the bed beside my mother. I stopped yelling and little by little everyone calmed down. And father went back to normal and started tidying the room: when one is under extreme pressure getting back to carrying out a routine task somehow always seems to help calm one down.

My parents were exceptionally beautiful, although in very different ways. My father, Andrei Astafiev, was slim and neat, with a dark complexion, curly black hair and the eyes of a gazelle. He was a man of integrity, persistent, often reserved, but if he did smile his smile was charming. My mother, Ephrosinia Maslikova (later Astafieva), was plump, white-faced, with dimples in her cheeks. Everyone who met her was immediately captivated by her wonderful charm. My father loved my mother throughout his life. They married in 1929 when she was 15 and by the marriage he saved her from exile to the unknown and, therefore, frightening Nadym in the far-away North where, in 1929, all my mother's family, including her parents, were driven by the Bolsheviks and died. Only my mother, who had quite unexpectedly become my father's wife, survived. My father's family had also perished long before my birth – in Georgia, that land of plenty, where they found themselves by fate in 1930.

As the Russian poet Zinaida Gippius put it, poetry is a kind of prayer. Those who understand our prayer will also understand our sorrow. Marcel Proust once said that creative work helps us to regain the lost time.

'Beauty will save the world'
The Idiot, Fyodor Dostoevsky

The Battlefield

A blank sheet of paper is my battlefield,
A pen is my revolver,
Writing is my rejection of the slow peace,
My attempt to be free of the galley chain.

I feel with my skin, with my nerves, with my whole self
The loss of the times
That were stolen and buried in a cage,
A night–time marsh watchman.

It is hard to look into the overstrained depths,
You will be sucked in and never break free.
But what can you understand now
Without someone who was forced into the depths?

At the end of my days,
I endeavour with my last bit of strength
To penetrate the remote centre of the night
Which once hid the light from me.

I may not be able to endure it, I may collapse,
And die on my journey,

But then I will give the one who follows me
The right to be oneself and believe in a miracle:

Everyone will be saved – by beauty –
As the incomparable Fyodor foretold,
To which idea I always pray.
Oh, Lord, hear my prayer for everybody!

1940

A Snowflake

A three-year-old girl sat in the kitchen on the newly-planed wooden table looking attentively through the window. It was snowing but the sun was shining brightly. It was February: snowy, bright, resonant.

The girl was looking curiously through the window as it was being covered with white. Big snowflakes were slowly landing on the window glass and sticking to it.

The girl pressed her finger against the glass trying to catch the snowflakes but was surprised to see a thin current of water flowing from under her finger. She expected to see the long-awaited snowflakes on her finger but she saw water instead . . . Where was the snowflake? She wanted so much to get the beautiful snowflake. She wanted to show it to her Mother when she at last came home from work.

Both of the girl's parents worked all day long. All three members of the family lived at a small railway station in far, far-away Siberia. Father was the station-master and Mother worked in the station snack-bar.[1] Father's younger brother, Tima, also lived with them. He was very young and as handsome as the girl's father. Tima loved his niece Tamara, who was called Toma for short. The girl always believed that she had been given that name because of her

---

[1] The station was in the small village of Petrovka in the Altaiski Krai district of southern Siberia, not far from the borders of China and Mongolia. The rivers Biya and Katun flow through the area close to Petrovka before converging to form the river Ob, over three thousand miles long, one of the great rivers of the world.

closeness to Tima. And, because Tima adored his niece little Toma, and the girl felt the same tender love for her handsome young uncle, they were both often called Toma-Tim or Tima-Tom.

Toma also loved her mother, whose voice always seemed divine. Her mother's smile was absolutely beautiful and made delightful dimples in her cheeks; Mother's hands were so warm, gentle and loving. They could not be compared to any other hands. The girl always reached out for Mother's hands.

The girl adored her father, Andrei, too. With his black curly hair he was very handsome. He was in love with the girl's mother all his life. He had married Mother when he was nineteen and Mother was just fifteen years old. Father had been born into a large, very poor family. Mother's family was large as well and her parents worked in the church. In 1929-30, when the Bolsheviks started persecuting the church, Father made the fifteen-year-old Fro (Ephrosinia) come to his home so that he could save her from the Red Army. The soldiers had arrested all the rest of her family, loaded them on to horse-drawn carts in only the clothes they had on and sent them to Nadym (Nadym wasn't a town or even a village then, just a region in the far-away north). And there, in Nadym, they all died.[2]

Father's family was not persecuted as they were very poor and so were not considered dangerous by the authorities. But in those

2 In 1929, after defeating Trotsky in the power struggle in the ruling Communist Party that followed the death of Lenin in 1924, Stalin instituted the first of the Five-Year Plans which were intended to transform Russia from a backward, largely feudal and agricultural, country into a powerful modern industrial state. He began by a massive enforced collectivisation of agriculture and mass deportations of peasants to newly created industrial centres and forced labour camps. This was backed by a campaign of terror and intimidation. Those who were thought likely to resist or regarded as potential 'enemies of the Revolution' were treated particularly harshly. Karl Marx had called

days the clergy influenced the way people thought while the authorities had from the start denied anybody else the right to exercise influence over people's souls . . . So it was that my mother's grandparents were killed by the Soviets while they were trying to consolidate their power.

Father's parents were saved thanks to their poverty. The Soviets preferred to deal with the poor: they seemed easier to tame. As for the rich, they were eradicated; people of moderate means followed them. Priests were included in the list of enemies: one of the Soviet slogans was 'Religion is the opium of the people'.[3] And not only priests but everybody who worked for the church, no matter how lowly – people like my mother's parents – they were killed as well, together with their little children, in the unknown, far-off Nadym.

So my father Andrei saved my mother from the Soviet government's repression. But I, Toma, only learned all these details

---

religion 'the opium of the people' which disguises from people the true cause of their suffering and said that it must therefore be done away with. Only then would people be able to achieve real freedom and happiness. The Russian Orthodox Church was seen by the authorities as standing in the way of the realisation of the goals of the Communist Revolution and so people who supported the church were dealt with particularly harshly. Stalin himself later told Churchill that as many as ten million Russians died as a result of the implementation of the Five Year Plans during the 1930s, the enforced collectivisation and industrialisation of the country, which took place between 1929 and the start of the Second World War. That figure has been confirmed by later scholarship. Nadym is a region in the far north of Siberia which contained a vast complex of forced labour camps where up to two million people died. Today the Nadym region is estimated to contain up to twenty per cent of world's known oil reserves and many other valuable minerals. Tamara only learned the full story of what happened to her parents' families many years later.

3 'Religion is the opium of the people,' quoted by Karl Marx, who wrote 'Die Religion . . . ist das opium des volkes'

after I had grown up, got married, given birth to a son and been divorced. My parents kept the whole story secret for a very long time because they continued to be afraid of the Soviet authorities.

But the three-year-old Toma still continued to sit in the kitchen trying to catch snowflakes on the window pane and waiting for her Mother. When Mother finally came home from work she took off her coat, stoked up the oven and put the pot of washed potatoes into it. The oven quickly got hot and the house became warm. Toma sat watching her Mother thoughtfully and suddenly asked, 'Ma! Why do I have such a strange name?' Fro stopped, dried the sweat from her forehead and, after a pause, answered, 'Why strange?' she asked. 'Yes, it is unusual for our Altai. But your full name is Tamara, a name nobody uses here. So you are called Toma for short or – your affectionate pet name – Tomochka.'

The girl thought about this for a while and then asked: 'But who gave me this name?'

Mother said, 'Your father,' and then added, 'Tonight, at tea-time, I will tell you more. But now have the hot potatoes, drink some milk and – take a nap! Good?'

The girl nodded her head, got down on to the floor and, sitting on a stool, started peeling the boiled potatoes. She was biting off small pieces and drinking milk. After Mother's long absence this food seemed fabulously delicious. And later in the evening, having made herself comfortable on the low stool at her mother's feet, the girl listened to her story and both of them cried several times.

April 1929

The Story Told by Fro, the Girl's Mother

'It was before you were born. I was just fifteen and your father was nineteen. Your father Andrei loved me very much and when he heard what was happening to my family, how they were being loaded onto open carts and sent, without any belongings, to the far-away north, to Nadym, to save me from being sent with the rest of my family, he took me by the hand and led me to his home and said, "You will live here!" And so, in this way, without drawing attention to what he had done, I became your father's wife. He loved me very much and this was how he saved me from certain death.[4]

'Your father's family was very large: his parents Elizaveta and Alexei had thirteen children. As you might expect, when I became his wife his family became very near and dear to me. By that time all of my own family had been exterminated on Stalin's orders. We were very poor and all the sixteen of us lived in the

4 This was all that Tamara's mother told her at the time about the fate of her family. Later, when she had grown up, Tamara learned the full story. Fro's parents were relatively well off and had close connections with the Church - both things that made them enemies in the eyes of the Bolsheviks. Tamara's father's family, on the other hand, were poor and so not seen by the authorities as 'class enemies', which allowed them to escape deportation. Tamara's future father, Andrei, heard that Fro's family were being deported and he immediately went to their house, took Fro by the hand and led her back to his family's home. Once there, he simply announced to his family: 'She will stay here with us.' Later he went to the offices of the local Soviet authorities and registered Fro as his wife.

same small house, with the Russian stove in the middle.

'I got pregnant . . . You know, when one is young hunger and cold don't seem so frightening. We were very united and did our best to help Andrei's parents look after the younger ones.

'Then one day (it must have been in 1930) a stranger came to our house. I don't remember his name, and very few people in the village knew him – but we Russians are very hospitable. We invited him in to have tea with us and after tea he started telling us about a strange and wonderful country called Georgia, where apple trees and trees with strange orange-coloured fruit grow right in the streets. The Astafievs of all ages listened to him with great attention and interest. The stranger also told them that Georgia was a very warm country and that the women there wore dresses even at that time of year, when we in Siberia had snow.

'New ideas had always fascinated your grandfather Alexei and the idea of moving to this warm country called Georgia seemed terribly exciting. Just imagine! To live in a warm land, near the sea, the sea that not one of them had ever seen! That was how it all started. Much later, after many trials and much suffering, everybody – including grandfather Alexei – realised with deep bitterness that the decision to leave their home in Siberia had been a blunder. But, at that time, after hearing all the things that the stranger had told them, there was nothing that anyone could have done to stop him: Grandfather Alexei was stubborn and once he had made up his mind there was never anything that anyone could do to make him change it. So we sold our dilapidated house (our own house!) and our cow – the support of the family! – bought train tickets and, all of us, even the babies, left for Georgia. By that time I had given birth to Sasha; he was eleven months old.

'Common sense should have told us that this idea was sheer madness. But Grandfather Alexei was the head of the family and we all obeyed him. Besides, everybody was young: even Grandfather Alexei and Grandmother Elizaveta were only a little over forty. People used to get married early in those days and had as many children as God gave them.[5]

'At that time people did not have handbags or purses; women would hide their money in the bosom of their dresses and men kept their money in their pockets. Valuables were wrapped up in a piece of cloth, fastened with a pin and hidden in secret (as it seemed to us then) places. It never occurred to anybody that a stranger could ever reach the hiding places. We were all innocent and kind and thought other people were as well.

'So all seventeen members of the Astafiev family set off for the mysterious and, as they had believed, warm land of Georgia. It was the 1930s, by which time the Soviets had taken control of the whole of Siberia. Prosperous, well-established farms were ruined; many of the peasant families who had worked the farms took their guns and fled to the woods to resist. The poor peasants who remained were ruined either by crop failure or because the Soviets expropriated everything that mooed or clucked.[6] Some families, like mine, together with even their youngest children, were exiled from their native villages to the Far North, next to the Arctic Ocean.'

Mother kept repeating these words over and over again, re-telling her story and weeping; holding my breath, I sobbed violently

5 At that time people did not know about contraceptives and abortions were unheard of. That's why there were a lot of children, unlike present-day Russian families.

6 Although the Bolsheviks had seized power in Moscow, St Petersburg and most of European Russia in 1917 the civil war which followed the revolution lasted until 1921. The Bolsheviks did not complete the subjection of Eastern Siberia until 1922. The programme of collectivisation of agriculture, which entailed evicting both wealthy farmers and poorer ones and placing their farms under the control of workers' collectives, resulted in a massive drop in agricultural production and widespread famine across large areas of Russia.

too. Young as I was, I understood that, for some unknown reason, I had been deprived of the love of my relatives, especially of my grandmother Maria and grandfather Nikolai. At that time, when they were barely fifty years old, some very cruel person had ordered them to be killed. Whose order it was – I did not know then. But I felt that it was utterly unfair and unforgivable. When I saw my mother's tears and listened to her sorrowful story about the death of my brother Sasha and the sad wanderings of the large Astafiev family in search of the supposedly warm, kind land of Georgia, where wonderful orange-coloured fruit were available all year round, I could not help weeping along with my Mother. This was what I thought listening to the story then, when I was just three years old. And Mother went on to tell me how grandfather Alexei had sold his house and his cow, split the money into several portions, wrapped them in cloth and given them to each of the adult members of the family to keep safe. Then they had walked to the nearest railway station, bought tickets and headed for Georgia.

'Your brother Sasha was very pretty. He had fair curly hair and blue eyes. Your father Andrei and I kept on wondering how such an angel could have been born to dark-haired and black-eyed parents. In our railway carriage everybody admired Sasha and wanted to hold him and cuddle him. I was too young to understand how dangerous that could be for a baby. I was flattered by the general admiration for my child and did not see anything wrong with it. But as a result of being passed from one passenger to another while wearing only his vest Sasha caught a cold and became sick.

'We had to get off the train urgently in a town called Ochamchira[7] (a name which sounded strange to us) to try to find a doctor who could help little Sasha and save him. But . . . it was in

7 Ochamchira, a town on the north east coast of the Black Sea in what the Soviet government had declared was the autonomous Soviet

vain. No one helped us, we did not find a doctor and Sasha died in my arms. I was frozen with grief. Andrei's look was frightening. From that time on I have known that the most dreadful thing that can happen to a person is to lose their child! We found a cemetery, dug a grave with our bare hands and buried our first-born child wrapped in my skirt. Andrei had to drag me away from the grave; he was only able to persuade me to leave the cemetery by saying that his parents and their children were waiting for us at the station. I realised we had to go. Andrei carved a small cross with his knife, we placed it in the ground over the grave and left for the station. When we arrived the family was already tired of waiting for us.

'When they saw our faces swollen with tears they understood everything; besides, I no longer had Sasha in my arms. Grand-mother Elizaveta burst into tears, and the rest of the family followed. Everybody loved my first-born Sasha – you couldn't help loving him! I embraced my husband's parents and said, "Little Sasha was an angel, and angels do not live long on earth . . . " We felt even more bitter . . .

'Then, without any tickets, we made our way onto another train that was going to Georgia, that "promised land". We spread ourselves out around the carriage; the children curled up on the luggage racks and their parents and Andrei slept on the floor. It was on that train that all our money was stolen! How did it happen? Who did it? I have no idea. None of the adults (let alone the children) could ever imagine anyone being so cruel. We must have been so tired from the stress and all the discomfort that nobody felt the thieves do it.'

'And what happened next?'

'We reached the sea, got off the train and stood on the platform

Republic of Abkhazia within the Soviet Republic of Georgia. Today the independence of the region remains the subject of an on-going dispute which in recent years has seen repeated outbreaks of fighting between Abkhazia and Georgia.

for a long time with no idea where to go. I do not even remember the name of the city. And then we walked until we saw a river with a concrete bridge over it. So we settled down and made our home under the bridge.

'Andrei's younger sister, Anna, and I were sent to raise some money by begging. But no one, not a single person, gave us anything. Soon Andrei fell seriously ill with malaria. It was damp and cold under the bridge; there were draughts and an awful lot of blood-thirsty mosquitoes. I think one of the mosquitoes must have bitten Andrei and infected him. He was shaking all over and had a fever. We had absolutely no idea how to help him. But then, fortunately, we saw a military patrol which was out looking for new recruits for the army. At that time our army was quite decent. As soon as they saw Andrei they decided to take him, too. We burst into tears: "Can't you see he is ill? Where are you taking him?"

'But the soldiers said, "Don't cry! Believe us, he will recover in the army. Here, under the bridge, he'll die." The women and children stopped crying and Andrei was put on a stretcher and taken away. At the last moment, before the soldiers carried him away, Andrei turned and whispered in my ear, "Please do not cry! I will find you, no matter what happens!" He loved me so much! And it was in the army that he was given treatment and recovered.'

And he did find her! Back in our Siberia, after my Mother had returned to live there with my Father's young brother Tima (ten) and his sister Anechka (thirteen). My Father found my Mother; he loved her and went on loving her for the rest of his life.

'Then something bad happened to our father, Alexei. He felt very ill and kept on disappearing and then coming back. At first we could not understand what was happening but then, when he moved down on to the edge of seashore and began to build a hut out of branches and twigs, it became clear that he was seriously ill and had left us so that he did not infect the rest of the family.

'By that time we had eaten all our food and I had to find a job as a farm-hand. I worked in the fields and gardens of local farmers until late at night. For my work I was paid a round loaf of bread and a jug of milk. I brought everything that I earned back to the family and divided the bread equally among all of them (leaving less for myself). Then I would pour the milk into a mug that we had found somewhere and gave it to the children and mother Elizaveta. As for father Alexei, he would only allow me to approach him to give him food. He would tell me to put the food on the ground and then leave – to avoid any contact with him. Later I would come back to pick up the mug and wash it in the sea.

'None of us had any medical knowledge but we soon guessed that Alexei had dysentery. After some time he died and all we could do was to throw his body into the sea. I was helped by Anna, who was just thirteen, and Tima, aged ten. Afterwards all three of us just sat on the ground and wept. I only came to myself when mother Elizaveta started complaining that she felt strange. We were terrified of being left without any parents and rushed to try to find a hospital. I found one and two first-aid men came and took Mother away to hospital. We did not know what was wrong with her, what illness she had.

'After my work each day at the farm I used to run back to the children to give them some bread and milk and then run to the hospital to see mother Elizaveta. This continued for a few days and then one day when I walked into her hospital ward I saw that her bed was empty. I understood immediately. I went and found the nurses and they told me matter-of-factly, "She died; her body was buried in the sea." Crying, I said a silent prayer for her and Alexei's souls and then went back to the children, all in tears.

'I should tell you that by then, out of all our large family, there were only three people left: Tima, Anna and me. The younger children had died one after the other. We had buried them, but I don't remember where. There was also my husband, Andrei –

somewhere in the army – and there were the three of us, under the bridge. I decided we must leave at once and somehow or other make our way back to our native land, to Altai in Siberia. I was so terrified that I might lose Tima and Anna as well that nothing on earth was going to keep me in that inhospitable, unfriendly and cruel Georgia. I realised that all of us, especially Andrei's father Alexei, had been lured there by the foolish tales told by that stranger. We Siberians were too credulous and believed that people in the rest of the world were as kind-hearted as we were. Georgia had indeed turned out to be a rich land where orange-coloured fruit, called tangerines and oranges, really did grow in people's gardens and where apple-trees were full of wonderful apples. But this fertile land was inhabited by evil and greedy people who were only kind to their friends and people they knew well. As for strangers, the local people treated them like serfs, farm hands, and gave them no sympathy or help. This is how it was.'[8]

With these words my Mother finished her story. And I know that she did not invent a single word of her terrible tale: she had lived through all those events and was soaked with tears as she recalled the death of her little Sasha and the barbarian funerals of Andrei's parents and nearly all of the members of the large Astafiev family.

'My daughter, you asked me about your name, which is so unusual in Siberia. It's all very simple! When your father Andrei

8 Georgia had been an independent kingdom until 1783 after which it became part of the Russian Empire. During the 1917 Revolution, although there were many Georgian members of the Bolshevik Party, other Georgians tried to seize the opportunity to re-establish Georgia's independence. However their uprising failed and in 1922 Georgia was incorporated into the USSR. Although Stalin himself was a Georgian, in the early 1930s many Georgians still hated the Russians and the thousands of hungry people who had fled south to Georgia in search of food and work.

was in the army hospital he often heard the name from other people. Someone (who must have been a well-educated person) told him about the Georgian author Shota Rustaveli and his exciting, captivating book called *The Knight in the Panther's Skin*. The book described a Georgian queen Tamara (Thamar) and Andrei loved the name and remembered it. That is why, when you were born, your father insisted on giving you this name.'[9]

Actually, almost nobody ever called me by my full name. Instead I always heard people calling me: Toma, Tomochka. And Father called me Tomik. My uncle Tima did not use any names at all except 'My sweetie'. He even took me with him when he went out on dates: after my Mother had wrapped me in a warm blanket, he would take the bundle containing 'his sweetie' and go out on a date! Mother would ask him, 'Where are you taking her? She will be a burden to you!' But he would always reply proudly, 'My sweetie will never be a burden to me!' And he would take the wrapped up bundle which was me and go out on his date. And nobody laughed at him – on the contrary, everybody admired him and the baby. Of course, I only learned about all this later, from my mother.

---

9 Shota Rustaveli (1172-1216) is widely regarded as Georgia's greatest poet. His epic poem 'The Knight in the Panther's Skin' is the Georgian national epic. It tells the story of a knight who, after many adventures both natural and supernatural, rescues his beloved from captivity and saves his country and his queen from usurpers. Rustaveli dedicated the poem to Queen Tamar. Tamar, also T'amar, Thamar or Tamara, born in around 1160, ruled Georgia from 1184 until her death in January 1213. She was the first woman to rule Georgia in her own right. The period of her rule is known as the Georgian Golden Age. Her reign saw Georgia win a series of astonishing military victories over enemies who had seemed much more powerful than Georgia. Tamar was very devout and was canonised by the Georgian Orthodox Church. She abolished the death penalty and all forms of torture in Georgia.

top left: Tamara's father and mother
top right: Tamara's uncle Tima
lower left: Tamara's aunt Anna (her father's sister)
lower right: Tamara's parents *c.*1944

top left: Tamara's mother
top right: Tamara's father
below Tamara with her parents *c.*1944

The Name

I was given a queen's name
Thus my solitude was predestined.

Tsarinas have never been entitled to family happiness
Though they may have experienced the mirage of love.

They would rule their lands with zeal;
And because of the need to always see ahead
Would support themselves wherever they went
Keeping their inner light hidden deep within their souls.

The world would bow down to them,
Groaning and moaning,
Oft times lying at their feet.

Tsarinas could never believe anyone
And, to be certain,
Smote the heads of those
Who were truly loyal.

Their loneliness was like a shining halo
Glistening and spilling light around their heads,
But there was emptiness
Both behind their thrones
And before them.

Their pedestals are strong and high.
People distance themselves from them,
Trying to avoid sin.

1941

When the war broke out in 1941 Father was still the station master. He was certainly subject to call-up but they did not send him to the front because he was doing important war work dispatching endless numbers of trains: either to the west, carrying Siberians who were going to defend Moscow, or to the Urals to where military establishments were being evacuated from the west, or dispatching trains carrying grain from Siberia to the war-torn areas in the west. Tima, who was then nineteen, was called up and sent to an artillery school in Krasnoyarsk and, after completing his training, was immediately sent to the front. My beloved, strikingly handsome uncle, Lieutenant Timofey Astafiev, died a glorious death on July 28, 1944. He did not live to see the victory in 1945, just ten months later. He was buried in a common grave in the Ukraine; his name was included in the Memorial Book of those who died in the war. Many years later I went to The Great Patriotic War Memorial Museum in Moscow and entered his name into the electronic Memorial Book, recording the dates of his birth (April 1922) and his death (July 1944).[10]

10 Timofey Astafiev was one of more than 20 million Russians who died during the Second World War.

7 May 2005

To the memory of Lieutenant Tima Astafiev who perished at the age of twenty-two near the town of Smely (Ukraine) in April 1944. We have never found my young uncle's grave: neither his elder brother Andrei (my father), nor I, Tima's niece.

In spring trees look like the curly hair of the Earth . . .
The song of birds rises higher every day . . .
Today we celebrate the sixtieth anniversary of Victory,
The same Victory, with bitter tears and resounding laughter.
Christ looks down upon us
Blessing human Memory
Pulsing through many minds
Eternally,
Appealing for the joy of wonders.

Commentary

After the war Stalin announced the first of a new series of five-years plans. These were intended to rebuild the war-shattered country, create new homes and establish modern industries with which to build up the Soviet Union's economic strength and protect its international position. Whole new cities and industrial complexes were established on virgin sites. Although much of the heaviest and most menial work was performed by slave labourers, convicts and political prisoners, including Russian soldiers who had fought in the war but had the misfortune to be taken prisoner by the Germans (making them traitors in the eyes of the authorities) and even some former partisans, imprisoned after the war as 'unreliable', the mass of new construction sites also led to the creation of thousands of new, well-paid jobs in the construction industry for those prepared to move home to take them. Tamara's father, Andrei, eager to better the lot of his family, gave up his job on the railway and moved with his wife and Tamara to a better paid job as a construction manager on one of these newly created industrial sites. This would be first of a series of moves during the next few years.

1945

Back in Georgia – Peaches in Rustavi

The first city we moved to from Siberia was Rustavi in Georgia. The city had just been established and a metallurgy plant and rolling mill were under construction.[11] It was there that Father worked. We lived in a big, nice room on the ground floor, which had a huge veranda. I went to school, into the first form. The climate in Rustavi was very warm and we schoolchildren always wore shorts. We didn't have satchels and so instead used string bags to carry our textbooks to school. Boys and girls studied together. Sometimes the boys picked on the girls but most of time everyone was very friendly.

One day something happened on our veranda which made a deep impression on me. There was a large bowl of peaches on the desk close to the window. I was sitting at the desk doing my homework. All of a sudden a man wearing striped clothes appeared and said to me, 'Little girl, don't be afraid, I am not going to do anything nasty to you. Please, just give me some peaches!' At first I was terrified, but then I nodded my head and muttered, almost under my breath, 'Of course! Take them! We have plenty!' The man started rapidly stuffing peaches into his pockets and eating them at the same time. He must have been in a hurry and the only thing he said to me before he disappeared was, 'Thank you very

11 Construction of the plant had started in 1944 to process iron ore from nearby Azerbaijan. The original city of Rustavi in southeast Georgia had been completely destroyed in 1265 by Tamerlane the Great, the Muslim warlord, born near Samarkand in what is today Uzbekistan, and was re-founded by Stalin during the Second World War. Tamara's father, Andrei, moved to Rustavi with his family early in 1945.

much, girl!' Later, that evening, when I told my parents about the stranger Mother could not help crying: she was so frightened for me. Father tried to comfort her, 'Come on, nothing awful has happened . . . ' Much later I learned that the metallurgy plant was being built by prisoners, so probably the man was one of them.[12]

A Wood Pink

My family never had a *dacha* (a summer cottage). Like so many other families, we were poor (although somehow we did manage to make both ends meet). So during the long school summer holidays I was usually sent to a children's camp (they were called 'Pioneer Camps').[13] While we were living in Rustavi, in Georgia, I was sent to a camp quite a long way from home. I have only good memories of that camp. I was eight and I felt at home there. Our stay at camp was over and we campers were in buses on the way back to Rustavi along the narrow Georgian Military Road which twisted between the mountains above a steep cliff.[14]

12 The existence of slave labour camps, containing millions of convicts and political prisoners of all kinds, was officially hushed up by the Soviet authorities, but rumours about them were rife. The full truth only really started to emerge after Stalin's death. Tamara's mother not only feared that the convict might harm her daughter, she was also afraid that if Tamara was seen giving food to a convict she and the whole family might be in trouble with the authorities.

13 The Young Pioneer Organization of the Soviet Union was the state's mass youth organisation for children aged ten to fifteen.

14 The Georgian Military Road: the historic name for a major route through the Caucasus from Georgia to Russia. It was built by the Russian military at the end of the eighteenth century, after the signing the Treaty of Georgievsk in 1783 under which Georgia became a Russian protectorate. In 1801 Tsar Alexander I ordered improvements to the road to facilitate troop movements and communications – hence its name.

From time to time the buses would stop to let the children rest and breathe in some fresh mountain air. During the stops our chaperones kept a watchful eye on us. But during one of the stops I went right up to the cliff edge and looked over. Down below, some feet below the road level, I saw a beautiful, bright wood pink. All of a sudden, the ledge where I was standing collapsed, and took me with it! Several of the chaperones rushed to the edge of the cliff and stood looking down at me, terrified: I was hanging below the ledge, with my foot wedged against a small tree that was directly below me. One of the men lay down on the cliff edge and stretched out his hand, holding a stick. I grabbed hold of the stick and felt them start to drag me up. As I got nearer to the top of the cliff other people grabbed hold of me by my head and shoulders and at last heaved me up. Everybody was crying and hugging me. They even forgot to tell me off. I was crying, too, but in my hand I was holding the wood pink that had so nearly caused me to plunge into the dreadful abyss. I couldn't remember how I had managed to pick the wood pink, but there it was, in my hand.

After a while everybody calmed down and we got back on to the buses. By the time we arrived at the bus station in Rustavi it was late at night. The chaperones put mattresses down on the floor for us and we went to sleep. In the morning our parents came to pick us up. When Mother found me and woke me up I was still holding the wood pink and proudly showed it to her. On the way home my parents learnt where and how I had got it. At home I put my flower in a glass of water. Wild flowers live a long time . . .

1946

Tallinn

Everywhere that my father worked he was respected and appreciated. He was hard-working, very reliable and neither drank nor smoked. On top of which it was virtually impossible to quarrel with him: his peacefulness and friendliness helped to solve any problems that arose. That's why the authorities always wanted to work with my father. Wherever his bosses were sent Father, together with his family, always followed them. In some places the living conditions were not too bad, but in other places they were far worse. Yet somehow we coped with the difficulties. Father was in love with my Mother and they both adored me. So I grew up in a loving family and my parents shared their love with the other people around them. It was always like that. I am now old, but my memories of my parents still warm my heart and help me to keep going.

Our second 'post-Siberian' city was Tallinn, the capital of Estonia.[15] The old city of Tallinn is very beautiful and surrounded with a fortress wall. In the centre of the city stands the town hall, with a tall tower topped by a weathervane called Old Toomas, the symbol of Tallinn. All the streets in the old quarter are paved with cobble-stones which are so smooth that women in high-heels can easily walk in them. Most of the old 'historic' Soviet films were made in Tallinn.

After the city of Rustavi Tallinn seemed to be rather cold. But it was extremely beautiful, with lots of old houses that looked like medieval castles. I enjoyed walking between the city's famous

---

15 The family moved to Tallinn during the winter of 1945–6.

ancient towers, each topped with weathercocks shaped like guards. In the old quarter there were lots of small shops which seemed very nice to visit . . . until one started speaking Russian. Almost all Estonians ignored you if you spoke in Russian.[16]

Many years later I returned to my beloved Tallinn to visit some good Russian friends of my parents who were living in the very centre of the city. Of course, I yielded to the temptation to visit the same nice shops in the city but now I spoke to shop assistants only in English. I remembered all too well that silent post-war Estonian attitude to even the smallest request made in Russian and did not want to experience the same unpleasant feeling again. So I used English (I thank Mark, my English language teacher at my school in Moscow who taught me fairly good English pronunciation).

When we arrived in Tallinn we lived in a long, single storey bunk house where each family occupied one room. It was always very cold in that house, the chill wind off the Baltic Sea seemed to blow straight through the walls. This was during the very hard immediate post-war period when there was not enough food and children often went hungry. I was no exception. But my aunt Anna, who at that time was working in a hospital as a cleaner, managed to help me: after school I would often run not home to our cold house but to Aunt Anna's hospital where she would have saved some buckwheat porridge for me. She would watch me as I

16 Animosity between Russians and Estonians went back many centuries, but reached a new pitch of intensity in 1939 when, at the start of World War II, after the signing of the Nazi-Soviet Non-Aggression Pact, Soviet troops marched into Estonia and occupied it. When Hitler attacked Russia in 1941 German troops drove the Russians out of Estonia but later in the war the Red Army recaptured it. From then on, until the fall of the Soviet Union, most Estonians hated Russians, regarding them as occupiers. To this day relations between Russia and Estonia remain strained.

was eating and quietly cry . . . My aunt always tried to live close to her elder brother Andrei, especially after the war which had taken away their brother Tima.

I was now in the second form. After school all the children living in our bunk house would play, running up and down the long central corridor of our bunk house, not wearing proper warm clothes. That was how I caught a cold along with bilateral otitis[17]. The doctor who used to come to that awful wind-blown barracks to treat me implored my father to try his utmost to move us to a decent, brick-built house as soon as possible. But we did not manage to move until a year and a half later, when our family was given two small rooms on the third floor of a big three-storey building. The third room in our flat had been allocated to a woman who never lived there, so we were the only tenants. It was unprecedented luck: the flat had a kitchen, a lavatory and even a bathroom. And, most important, it was warm! Actually, our flat in Tallinn was the most comfortable place that we lived in in all the years when we were travelling around the country. We even had a telephone!

One day when I was alone at home the telephone rang. I picked up the receiver and there was a man on the other end. The conversation that followed was unexpectedly odd. Throughout my childhood and later, during the long years of my adult life, people said that I had a beautiful sounding voice. The man on the other end of the line realised that he was talking to a little girl and greeted me in a very polite manner. Then he said, 'Girl, your voice is very melodious, who do you inherit it from?' I said, 'From my mother.' He told me that he was twenty-eight years old

17 Bilateral Otitis is an ear condition, especially common in young children, which is often brought on by catching a cold or other infection. The symptoms include acute pain, fever and vomiting. It can lead to loss of hearing.

and a Captain First Rank.[18] He asked when my parents were expected to be home from work and I told him. I talked to the stranger calmly and confidently as I had got used to speaking on the telephone back in Siberia where Father often used to phone me during the day so that I would not feel lonely.

In the evening there was another call and it was Mother who picked up the receiver. The same voice confessed that he 'had fallen in love' with her daughter's voice and asked for her permission to visit us while his ship was in the roads. Mother said he could and that was how, at the age of eight, I became acquainted with the twenty-eight-year-old Captain First Rank. The Captain was absolutely charming. Whenever his ship was in the roads he would visit us. When the time came when we had to leave Tallinn we were all very sad. Unfortunately, we did not know the new address that we would be going to and so we lost touch with the Captain First Rank. But my memories of the amazing Captain grew into a love for all sailors who wore the beautiful shoulder straps and dirk of the Russian naval uniform. That must have been my first, almost adult love! But, like many others later, it came to nothing.

Just across the road from where we lived there was a church which my mother often took me to. And two blocks away there was a proper cinema called *Forum* where I used to spend all my lunch money. A little further on there was a splendid park called Kadriorg where our whole family used to go for walks. When it was warm enough we bathed in the sea (in the Gulf of Finland). I just could not afford to catch another cold!

As I said, I saved my daily school lunch money and, instead of buying food, used it to go to the *Forum* cinema where they showed foreign films: *The Thief of Bagdad, Lady Hamilton*.[19] At

18 Captain First Rank: A senior officer in the Soviet Navy roughly equivalent in rank to a commodore in the Royal Navy.
19 Known as *That Hamilton Woman* in the UK.

the age of eight I met Deanna Durbin in *His Butler's Sister* and will remember forever the romantic Gipsy song *Two Guitars* which she sang in her charming, slightly broken, Russian.[20] I fell in love with the American actor Robert Taylor and his beautiful companion played by Vivien Leigh (in *Waterloo Bridge*) who could not get over her disgrace and jumped into the Thames from the bridge.[21]

I have remembered the final sequence of the film all my life: handsome Robert Taylor, standing on Waterloo Bridge, caressing with his fingers the good luck charm given him by his lover. And I also remember my amazement over the stunningly beautiful Vivien Leigh's performance opposite Laurence Olivier in *Lady Hamilton*. I am so grateful for my youthful years in the city of Tallinn where, back in 1946, I had the opportunity to see those wonderful foreign cinema masterpieces which helped me to form my ideal of what a charming woman should be.

But I was not influenced by these hit foreign movies alone but also by the best of Soviet cinema: I watched some good Russian films, like *The Tale of the Siberian Land*[22] directed by the famous film director Ivan Pyriev in 1947.[23] Brilliant Russian actors starred in it: Marina Ladynina,[24] Boris Andreev, Vera Vassilieva, Vladimir Druzhnikov, Vladimir Zeldin. My father took me to the cinema

---

20 A medley of Russian songs, arranged by Max Rabinowitz, was included in the film.

21 Actually, she throws herself in front of an on-coming lorry on the bridge.

22 Also known as *Symphony of Life* and *The Ballad of Siberia*.

23 Ivan Pyriev was one of the most successful Soviet film directors of the Stalin era, his musical comedies rivalling in popularity those of Grigori Alexandrov. Pyriev was awarded the Stalin Prize no less than six times. Pyriev, like Tamara, was born in the Altaiski Krai region of Siberia, close to the river Ob.

24 Ivan Pyriev's wife.

to see it immediately after it was released; it was on at the luxurious Tallinn Drama Theatre which had special boxes and armchairs. At the same theatre I also saw, thanks to my father, a divinely wonderful film based on one of Bazhov's fairy tales, *The Stone Flower*.[25] The wonderful flower was made of semi-precious stones by a Urals craftsman called Danila. I sat motionless looking at the proud beauty of the Lady of the Copper Mountain played by Tamara Makarova and the amazingly handsome craftsman Danila, played by Vladimir Druzhnikov.[26]

At that time I did not know anything about film crews and people such as cameramen or production designers. But I clearly remember my delight at the scenes deep underground beneath the mountains. My amazement was so great that for some years I regularly walked in my sleep. Mother used to be terrified when she saw me get up in the middle of the night from my bed where I was sleeping and wander around the room without touching anything. She said I would smile, say something, open the lavatory door (without going in), switch on the light . . . and then I would go back to my room where, near my bed, there was a stool for my clothes. For some reason, I would not get back into bed but curled up on the stool like a kitten. Mother was afraid of my night wanderings and was going to put a basin filled with water in my way: someone had told her that I would step into the basin and as a result of the shock my somnambulism would stop. But Father managed to talk Mother out of the idea. Instead, I was taken to the doctor who said that it was typical of children with delicate, highly sensitive, vulnerable nervous systems. He added that I would

25 Pavel Bazhov, a Russian writer best known for his collection of fairy tales *The Malachite Casket*, based on the folk-lore of the Urals, which was published in the Soviet Union in 1939. The film, made in 1946, was directed by Alexander Ptushko.

26 The two films were the first colour movies to emerge from the USSR, which may be why Tamara remembers them so well.

continue walking in my sleep until the age of sixteen and that after that my sleepwalking would disappear. He also praised my parents for doing without the basin of water as the nervous stress caused by the sudden contact with cold water would make me stutter for the rest of my life. The doctor turned out to be correct: it all stopped when I was sixteen.

1947

Baku

From Tallinn we moved on to the Azerbaijani capital, Baku. My strongest memory of Baku is the loud cries of the street peddlers: '*Matsoni! Matsoni!*' *Matsoni* is a thick sour fermented milk, which was very tasty!

By this time I was in the fourth form and was a good pupil. In the fourth form pupils had to take their first school exams and I worked hard to get ready for them – although I often hid a book of fairy tales (*One Thousand and One Nights*) under the textbook on my desk. Nevertheless, I did very well in the exams. Mother used to bring tiny paper bags of sugar sand to my room and say to me, 'Have it all now – it will help you to be cleverer!' Later I found out that to get the precious sugar, Mother would go to the market to exchange some of her clothes for those small bags of sugar.[27]

27 Throughout the 1940s, 1950s, and on and off until the collapse of the Soviet Union, there were food shortages in the USSR in spite of the government's repeated attempts to boost food production. One of the commodities affected was sugar. However in 1961, after Castro's revolution in Cuba and the imposition of a trade embargo by the USA, the USSR entered into a trade agreement with Fidel Castro under which the USSR agreed to import eighty-per-cent of Cuba's sugar production in return for supplying Cuba with agricultural

In Baku we lived in a room with a balcony. Directly below the balcony there were some big mulberry trees. In the autumn they were covered with dark-purple sour-sweet berries, similar to raspberries. All the children would hang little baskets round their necks and climb high up into the trees to pick the mulberries. Their mouths quickly became stained dark purple!

Our flat in Baku had double bunk beds. One afternoon I was asleep on the top bed when I was woken up by someone very heavy crawling on top of me. I recognised the man: he was a distant relative of ours. I was very frightened even though I did not understand what was happening. I was pretty and attractive but I certainly was not Nabokov's *Lolita*! I flinched when I felt something sticky and stinking on my bare feet . . . I remembered the handsome and noble Captain First Rank who had hardly dared even to breathe in my direction. And now here was this repulsive animal who wanted something of me. I started fighting, biting, wriggling like a cat. I managed to jump down from the bunk and burst into tears. The man was frightened by my tears and ran away. I kept asking myself what it was . . . , what had happened. I vaguely knew that men and women had relationships but at that time I had no understanding of their deeper meaning. One thing I did realise was that I was missing the tenderness of the Captain from Tallinn. But, as my life was to prove, tenderness was something I would always lack . . . Possibly that episode in Baku was the reason for the endless lonely days and nights that I was to experience in my adult life.

---

machinery and other goods vital for the island's economic development. Sugar sand is a rather coarse sugar which has been refined less than white, granulated or caster sugars. Tamara's mother was anxious to ensure that her daughter received sufficient nourishment.

1948-1950

Gomel

A big dairy and beef processing factory was under construction in the city of Gomel in what was then the Soviet Republic of Byelorussia (today Belarus) and Father was invited to work on the project. In Gomel we stayed with a very nice lady called Vera Zakharovna. She had two daughters, Liolya and Natasha. They lived in a house with a small kitchen garden and an orchard. Liolya was living at home with her mother and Natasha was studying at a university in Minsk, the Byelorussian capital. Later Liolya also left home to become a medical student. I became good friends with Liolya and our friendship lasted for many years: when we moved to Moscow she used to come to see us, and I would go Minsk to see her. Our hosts in Gomel were kind, sincere, very friendly people and we felt at home there.

When we moved to Gomel I was eleven years old and went to a very good school where I spent my fifth and sixth school years. The school was a four-storey building with spacious classrooms and large windows. But for some reason the lavatories were outside in the school yard. They were a wooden shed divided into two sections: one for boys and one for girls. Inside there was a row of holes in the wooden floor. This toilet played me an evil trick: I caught typhoid fever from it. Two of us were infected. The other girl quickly died but I was saved by our school doctor. She recognised the disease at once, carried me back to my home in her arms and then called an ambulance. By her prompt action she saved my life. In hospital, where I spent a month, the school doctor's diagnosis was confirmed.

I was not allowed any visitors while I was in hospital: not my parents, my classmates, nor even my rescuer – the school doctor. But I did not feel lonely as every day I received a parcel from them – in each one there was a note full of love and tenderness. Love was what I most needed just then. When I started to get better I began doing my school work again which the school sent to the hospital and the nurses passed on to me. Mother used to bring notebooks, pens and ink-pots to the hospital for me (there were no ballpoint pens in those days).

I was in the fifth form when I caught typhoid. During my stay in hospital they had to shave all the hair off my head – right down to the scalp. When I got back home and was well enough to go back to school Mother said, 'You can't go to school like that, with your almost bald head. Put on a head-scarf'. I agreed. But when I got back to school the boys started chasing me: one or other would sneak up behind me and pull off my head-scarf and the rest of the boys would burst out laughing in the silliest manner. I got so bored with this that after a bit I took off the scarf myself and proudly walked past the boys who simply stood there with their mouths wide open. Strange as it may seem, nobody bullied me after that or laughed at my 'bald' head.

By then my hair was growing very quickly and, to my surprise, it was growing back curly. Now I had a new trouble: the boys were excited by my curls. Mother explained to me that this sometimes happened after typhoid fever – one's hair grew back curly after the illness. But it was impossible to explain this to every single boy. So, upset by my curls, I decided to fight them: I soaked my hair with water and then tried to smooth it out with a hot iron. It is a wonder that I did not scorch my hair! Gradually everybody got used to my new look and only my mother would say with a sigh, 'Nature is so unpredictable!' and kept on praying for me. She asked God to protect me from people's bullying and insults. I heard her praying, 'She is such a good, kind girl! Lord, please help her!' She used to repeat the last phrase three times.

1951

Moscow

Father had always wanted to move to Moscow, and there was a special reason for that: he wanted to give his daughter a higher education and, more than that, he wanted her to study in Moscow. At last his dream came true.

In the summer of 1950, when the school term was over, Father was summoned to Moscow: construction was beginning on the new Moscow State University in the Lenin Hills (formerly known as the Sparrow Hills).[28] To start with Father went to Moscow on his own, but later, in 1951, mother and I joined him. At first we lived in a bunk house but after a little while Father managed to get us a fifteen-square-metre room in a flat in a proper brick house. It was not at all luxurious but, still, the room had a window and a balcony. The name of the district where we lived had an endearing name, Novye Cheremushki (New Bird Cherry Trees).[29] And, it's true, there were a lot of bird cherry trees around.

Our flat was on the second floor and had three rooms. It was

28 Moscow State University was founded in 1755. During the Second World War, when Hitler's armies threatened Moscow, it had been evacuated to the east and after the war, after the university had returned to Moscow, the Soviet government decided that the university must be greatly enlarged and the student intake increased so as to help in the post-war reconstruction and development of the USSR. Construction of a huge new campus in the Sparrow Hills, then on the edge of Moscow, was begun in July 1949. The first students arrived on the new campus in 1952.

29 Noyve Cheremushki, a sought after district of Moscow about five miles southwest of the city centre.

meant for one family but . . . there were three families living in it: one in each room. Housing has always been a big problem in Moscow. It was not without reason that Mikhail Bulgakov wrote in his novel *The Master and Margarita:* 'Muscovites have been corrupted by the housing problem.'[30] But we were friends with our neighbours. Our fifteen-square-metre room did not leave much space for furniture. There was a wardrobe, a sofa and – between them – a big box made of plywood which Father had found somewhere. We put it on its side and turned it into my desk! The writing surface was on the top and I sat with my legs inside. In the bottom of the box there was also room for my toys.

In Moscow I went into the seventh form of School No. 638 and I studied there until I got my certificate of secondary education after the end of my year in the tenth form. I finished school with excellent marks in all the humanities and passable grades in the other subjects. In English I had a 'four' (a good mark). I was very sorry that English classes only began in the seventh form and we had just one class a week. Evidently, it never occurred to the people in the Ministry of Education that very soon English would become an international language. I enjoyed our English classes but to have English one hour a week – idiocy! But then, idiocy was typical of the Soviet education bosses.

Over the years there were several women teachers who made an unforgettable impression on me. In Tallinn it was Maria Alexandrovna who looked as though she could have been a teacher at the Smolny Institute;[31] in Gomel it was Yadviga Alexandrovna

30 In *The Master and Margarita* the Devil concludes that the housing problem is the source of the Muscovites' corruption. Private space has become privileged space and so a source of status and power, fought over and riddled with corruption, bribery and coercion.

31 The Smolny Institute for Noble Maidens, founded in St. Petersburg in accordance with a decree of Catherine II (the Great) in 1764, was Russia's first educational establishment for women and continued to

(she was of Polish origin); and in Moscow school No. 638 it was another Maria Alexandrovna, who taught us History.

It was at this school in Moscow, while I was in the seventh form, that I, like all the rest of the girls (at that time boys and girls went to separate schools), fell in love with our English teacher. I can still remember his fine features, his beautiful thin fingers, his height (he was very tall), and his light-brown corduroy coat.

Because I was in love with my teachers I memorised every single little thing that was typical of them. Most importantly, I learned from them by example (without them having to teach me) how sit attractively, how to cope with my gawky hands and feet, how to walk gracefully, to speak and to listen. Each one of them taught me something that was later to be of great help to me in my adult life.

Similarly, an indelible impression was made on me by all the women characters of the films I mentioned earlier. It was a rich school of life for a teenage girl. All those wonderful films, as well as Russian and Western literature, were not only a school of life but also a school in aesthetic appreciation and how to find joy through contact with the beautiful. In my teenage years I read all of Chekhov, Gorky, Leskov,[32] *The Forsyte Saga, Jane Eyre* . . . So it was both good Russian literature and Western literature that shaped the Tamara who years later would work at the Novosti Press Agency.

But let's get back to our life in Moscow.

I have always had a passionate love of the theatre. My desire to

function under the personal patronage of the Russian Empress until just before the 1917 revolution.

32 Nikolai Leskov (1831–1895), Russian novelist, short story writer, playwright and journalist (who also wrote under the pseudonym M.Stebnitsky) who was held in high esteem by Tolstoy, Chekhov, Gorky and many others for his style, experiments in literary form and ability to create a comprehensive picture of contemporary Russian society. His works include *Lady Macbeth of Mtsensk*.

become an actress burned inside me like a flame. And it was not for nothing that my father also wanted me to have such a career. In our room there was a radio perched high up on top of the wardrobe. In the evenings they often broadcast radio adaptations of theatre performances. I had an overwhelming desire to listen to them but Father had to get up very early in the morning, at seven or even six o'clock. Being an extremely punctual person, he used to get to work at eight instead of nine. So turning up the volume of the radio to listen to the plays was out of the question. But one day Mother somehow got hold of an earphone, connected it to the radio and from then on I listened to the 'radio theatre' almost every night without disturbing anybody.

Mother had also noticed my love for reading and somehow managed to buy a wonderful bookcase for me! She told me, 'Daughter, there is a bookstore nearby where they sell the collected works of different authors by subscription. At the beginning you only have to pay for the first and the last volume of each edition. Go there and subscribe, I will give you the money.' I was so excited! And did just as my mother told me.

A seamstress called Tamara Alexandrovna lived on the first floor of our house. She was very fond of French fashions and one of her friends used to regularly bring her beautiful fashion magazines. Sometimes Mother contrived to save some money and with it would buy me some beautiful fabrics. So Father's perfect taste (which he had imparted to Mother) plus French fashion equalled pretty dresses or suits made for me by the seamstress. As a result I always wore fashionable and beautiful clothes.[33]

33 The clothes sold in shops in the Soviet Union were notoriously drab and 'utilitarian' rather than stylish. Many people when they wanted something stylish, and could afford it, would buy materials and get a local seamstress or tailor to make clothes for them, based on fashions and designs that they found in fashion magazines which were often smuggled into the USSR from abroad.

1952

The Magic Lake

Tanya Chizh lived in the same communal flat as me in Novye Cheremushki in Moscow. She lived with her mother Maria Petrovna in the same way as I lived with my parents.[34] Maria Petrovna was a charming woman and very interesting to talk to. But, for some reason, the atmosphere in their family was not friendly, unlike in our family, where all three of us adored each other and lived together in peace and harmony. It seemed strange to me that a daughter could be so hostile towards her mother but I did not try to interfere in their relationship, and accepted them as they were. I liked Maria Petrovna: her neatness, tidiness, the way she dressed and applied her make-up, and especially the way she applied her lipstick so as to make her naturally nice-shaped lips look even prettier. Tatiana, on the other hand, did not like anything about her mother; she used to sniff scornfully when she saw Maria Petrovna applying her lipstick. Tanya also teased me for admiring her mother.

Maria Petovna's parents lived in Leningrad, so Tanya and I often travelled there for the White Nights.[35] Oh, the White Nights, the delight and enjoyment that Muscovites never know! Those

34 Petrovna is a female patronymic, a name derived from the father's side of the family, which is commonly used in Russia. The male name will often finish with '-evich' e.g. Georgi Nickolaevich. In Russia it is an official element in a person's name. Among close friends of older age, patronymics can be used without one's first name.

35 The White Nights in St Petersburg last for about a month from the middle of June until the middle of July. During this period streets are not artificially lit at nights, because it does not get dark at all. On the longest day the sun stays in the sky for nineteen hours, but even when it sets there is still enough light to read by.

nights were unforgettable! Every night we would wander around the completely light and heavenly beautiful city. Then we would return to Tanya's grandparents' flat (of course, they were asleep by that time), sit down on the old chest in the corridor and whisper, whisper, whisper . . . Girlish dreams and memories of something very intimate . . . We enjoyed, no – we indulged – in our talks. At that time we were fourteen or fifteen years old – just the right age to dream and even daydream . . . !

For the summer Tanya's grandparents usually went to the country, to the village of Toksovo[36] where they had a small summer cottage (a *dacha*).[37] The main attraction of Toksovo was the lake of the same name: Toksovo. It was not just a lake, it was like something from a fairy tale, a water kingdom where we could swim at night! When Tanya and I entered that magic world we felt we were naiads. Tatiana was an especially skillful naiad as she could swim and dive perfectly. As for me, I could only swim near the bank: with my chronically delicate ears (following that cold I had caught in Tallinn) I could not risk doing the tricks Tanya did as she enjoyed the clean and gentle water. The moon was reflected in the lake, adding a further touch of magic to the atmosphere, making our souls rejoice even more. We used to spend nearly every night swimming in that magic lake; our pleasure is hard to put into words!

In the morning we would eat strawberries and fresh cucumbers straight from the kitchen garden – the cucumbers seemed to crunch so loudly that it seemed they could be heard all over the

36 Some twelve miles north of Leningrad (St Petersburg) in an area of lakes, forests and old traditional wooden houses, famed for its beauty and its profusion of wild flowers, fruit and fungi.

37 *Dacha* is a Russian word referring to seasonal or year-round second homes, often located in the outskirts of Soviet and post-Soviet cities. *Dachas* are very common in Russia, and widespread in most parts of the former Soviet Union. It is estimated that about fifty-per-cent of Russian families living in large cities have *dachas*.

village. When Tanya's short, grey-haired grandmother called us for breakfast we would race each other to sit down at the table in the yard, in the open air. The cottage was surrounded by a pine forest, so the air was clear and fragrant. Tanya's grandfather, who was nearly twice as tall as his wife, amazed us with his aristocratic bearing and noble manners. Each long summer day would be followed by another long summer night in the wonderful lake where we would swim, at one with nature, making strange wordless sounds of delight.

My one regret is that God allowed me to enjoy that precious gift just twice. My adult life in Moscow was about to begin . . . But I will always remember Toksovo with its magic lake; I will always be grateful to Maria Petrovna, Tanya and her hospitable grandparents.

1953

The Death of Stalin

On 6 March, 1953, when I was in the ninth form, all the pupils, from the first to the tenth forms, were summoned to the school assembly hall. Mournful music was playing. Then the Principal made an announcement which shocked everybody: 'On the fifth of March, Comrade Stalin passed away.' The children were confused and distressed, some started crying.[38] After the announcement our

---

38 At the time of his death, in 1953, Stalin was widely regarded as the 'Father of the Russian People', the leader who had saved them from defeat and then led them to victory in World War Two. The official bulletin announcing Stalin's death read: 'The heart of the comrade-in-arms and continuer of genius of Lenin's cause, of the wise leader and teacher of the Communist Party and the Soviet Union, has ceased to beat.' The true extent of Stalin's crimes only became known to the ordinary people of Russia some years later.

class returned to our classroom; no one left. A few girls (it was an all-girls' school) – me among them – decided to go to the House of the Unions where Stalin was lying in state in the Column Hall. Back at home I told my Father what I was planning to do and he tried to talk me out of going, but I had it my way and went with the other girls. Three of the five of us girls managed to pass through three security lines the police had set up around the approaches to the House of the Unions but then we were stopped at the fourth one.[39] The officers wrote down our names and then let us go home. It was a very cold March day and we were nearly frozen to death. When I got home I think Father was ready to beat me. But he just said in his strictest voice, 'Take a shower immediately and then go to bed!' And then he growled, 'You are grown-up! You ought to understand certain things and think more. Please do not be silly: you are a smart girl. You should praise the Lord that they let you go . . . ' Only years later did I understand the words he used, especially the last ones.[40]

39 After his death Stalin was embalmed and driven in a huge white hearse to the House of the Trade Unions, a few streets away from the Kremlin, and carried by pall-bearers to lie in state for three days in its great Column Hall. Millions of Russians flocked to the building to try to get one last glimpse of their former leader. The chaotic crush of people trying to get into the building was so great that the police were unable to control it and up to 500 people were trampled underfoot, crushed against lamp posts or suffocated.

40 People were very fearful of any contact with the Soviet police or KGB, but Tamara believes that her father's anger and concern for her went further than this common fear and arose from his sense that things were seriously wrong in the country.

Crowds gather to see the embalmed body of Stalin, lying in state in Moscow, 1953

1953-1955

A Concert by Georg Ots

After I left school I found a job as a carer in a kindergarten. I loved children and, more importantly, they loved me. I particularly remember one boy, who was two and a half years old, and used to fall asleep during meals with his spoon in his mouth. I would go quietly up to him, feed him and then put him to bed.

I worked in the kindergarten for about two months and after that I worked for several months as a laboratory assistant at my old school. By getting work experience in this way I hoped to improve my chances of being accepted to do a correspondence course at an institute of higher education.

At the same time I was always looking for ways to fulfil my artistic nature and so I enrolled as a student at a drama studio in the local community centre (such centres were and are still called Palaces of Culture in Russia). We staged plays and rehearsed poems to recite at parties and concerts given to mark Soviet holidays. Our artistic director at the Palace of Culture put my name forward to be the hostess at a big concert that was to be given by Georg Ots.[41] I was selected and, as a result, in 1953, aged just fifteen, I became the hostess at a concert given by one of the best loved singers in the Soviet Union in one of Moscow's most famous concert halls, the Column Hall in the House of the Trade Unions, the same hall where, a few months earlier, Stalin had lain in state and thousands

41 Georg Ots, 1920-1975. A revered and much-loved Russian operatic baritone who sang at the Bolshoi and many leading opera houses around the world. He also starred in a number of Soviet films. He was a noted interpreter of Schubert, Mussorgsky, Tchaikovsky and the folk songs of his native Estonia.

had struggled to try to get in to see him one last time. Mother put in an urgent order for me (with our seamstress friend) for a nice black pinafore dress and a spotted yellow blouse with balloon sleeves. She also asked a shoemaker to make me a pair of high-heeled shoes. The clothes were soon made for me by my namesake Tamara, the dress-maker who lived next door.

At that time my voice was clear and resonant and unspoilt by asthma. I seem to have been a good hostess because, when the concert was over, Georg Ots took me in his arms, lifted me off the floor and kissed me on both cheeks, to thank me for my work. The audience burst into applause. I was totally happy! This was my one and only big-stage performance.

And then . . . then I was summoned to the Lubyanka (the KGB headquarters) and asked about the shoemaker who had made the shoes for me! I told them that it was my mother who had placed the order for the shoes through someone she knew – and I added that it was impossible to buy shoes in the shoe shops: such shoes were completely unavailable![42]

They listened to me attentively, wrote something down and then let me go. They also paid a visit to the shoemaker and asked him to show them the last he had used to make my shoes and even the drawing of my foot. It must sound like madness or a bad nightmare, but it is true. That's how life was in the Soviet Union!

Our artistic director at the Palace of Culture was an experienced theatre director and he strongly advised me to enter a theatre school. Once, when I had recited a passage from Leo Tolstoy's *Anna Karenina* (a scene where Anna meets her son) I had seen

42 The shortages of luxury goods and the fact that things like smart, well cut clothes and fashionable shoes were virtually unobtainable in the Soviet Union gave rise to an extensive black market in such items imported illegally from the West. The Soviet authorities conducted repeated crack-downs on this illicit trade, backed up by a legion of informers and harsh punishments, but were unable to stamp it out.

people in the audience crying during my performance, so I came to accept our artistic director's advice and applied to get into the Shchukin Theatre Institute.[43] I went to the audition but when the famous actress Serafima Birman[44] asked me, 'Dear girl, has anyone ever told you that you have a squint?' I got terribly embarrassed, apologised and quietly left the room. And yes, for a long time afterwards I cried sitting on a bench in the Alexandrov Garden near the Kremlin.[45]

Our artistic director scolded me for my shyness. He said, 'You are so photogenic and talented, try the Film School!' But I didn't. However, I did make another attempt: I went to the audition at the Moscow Art Theatre Studio where the board of examiners included both famous actors and first-year students. I failed again but, after the audition, the first-year students surrounded me, encouraging me to try again the following year . . . But I did not.

My father was probably even more upset by my failure to get into a drama school than I was myself and continued to dream of me becoming an actress. I think I might have been a good actress if it had not been for my extreme shyness. However, in the meantime I had won a place on an extra-mural degree course with the Department of Russian Language and Literature at the Moscow Pedagogical Institute[46] and later found a job at the Sea Transport Publishing House.[47] Editing turned out to be interesting and even exciting work and so, after I had got married and had my

---

43 Shchukin Theatre Institute was one of the most prestigious drama schools in the Soviet Union and remains one of Russia's leading theatre schools.

44 Soviet theatre and film star, who starred as the chief villain in Eisenstein's *Ivan the Terrible, Part II*.

45 One of the most beautiful parks in Moscow.

46 Russia's leading teacher training institution.

47 The Sea Transport Publishing House was a Soviet publisher specialising in subjects related to the sea, ships and other technical books. After

son Sergei, I returned to my job at the publishing house. But I still longed for an even more interesting and exciting job and it would again be my father who helped me.

1957

Finding out about Love

1957 was the year of the Moscow International Youth Festival.[48] I was working at the Sea Transport Publishing House and my bosses chose me to represent Soviet youth at the Festival. I was delighted: two weeks of unexpected holiday accompanied with songs, dances, smiles . . . It was like a fairy tale! As it turned out, during all twelve days of the Festival I travelled with the delegation from Cyprus. We visited so many places together, met so many people.

Our neighbour, the seamstress, had made a strikingly beautiful printed cotton dress for me: fancy roses with green leaves on a dark-red background. The dress had a pretty low neckline and complimented my looks very well. Together with my black curls

starting work at the Sea Transport Publishing House Tamara continued her studies at the State Pedagogical Institute through its Correspondence Department. Much later, between 1982 and 1984, after she had left the Novosti Press Agency and gone to work at the Film Makers Union, Tamara completed a second degree, in photo journalism, at the Moscow Institute of Journalism.

48 The 1957 International Youth Festival held in Moscow, attended by more than thirty-four-thousand students and young people from more than one-hundred-and-thirty countries, was the sixth and largest of a series of festivals of international youth held in different capitals around the world and dedicated to international peace and friendship. The festivals started in 1947 and continue to this day at four yearly intervals.

the dress made me look like a Gypsy or a Greek girl . . . In the end I very nearly ran away to Cyprus – a handsome Cypriot courted me so ardently!

The following summer (1958) I was invited to spend my vacation in the south with a group of students from the Bauman Higher Technical School.[49] It was a hiking and camping holiday. The plan was for the group to travel on foot from Anapa[50] to Lake Ritsa[51] and then go on to Sochi[52] where we were to camp in tents for several days. They used a bugle to call the campers to meals and other events.

Two of the young men in the group flirted with me: one was tall and skinny, and always wore a straw hat and a neckerchief (in the Spanish fashion), the other was a strong, vigorous fellow with blue eyes. One day the bugle sounded and it was announced that we were going on an excursion to the botanical gardens. Everybody was happy except me: I was lying on a blanket beside my tent writhing with stomach ache. It was probably the result of over-indulgence in the local fruit. So everybody left and I stayed behind. Before leaving the two guys came over to me and asked,

49 Although not a student at the Bauman Higher Technical School, Tamara had friends there and it was they who invited her to join them on holiday. The Baumann Higher Technical School (today the Bauman University), founded in 1830, is the oldest, largest and most prestigious institution of higher technical learning in Russia. It concentrates above all on producing highly trained engineers and instrument makers.

50 A Soviet holiday and health resort on the northern coast of the Black Sea near the Sea of Azov.

51 A lakeside and forest resort high in the Caucasus Mountains of Abkhazia where Stalin had had one of his summer holiday dachas.

52 Sochi is a city on the Black Sea close to the border between Russia and Georgia (then one of the Soviet republics forming the USSR). It became a fashionable holiday resort during Stalin's time and he built what was to become his favourite holiday *dacha* there.

Tamara, about 1956

'What do you want us to bring back for you from the botanical gardens?' I said, 'A rose'. And, being very romantic, I added, 'I will marry the one who brings me the sweetest-smelling rose.' My statement was both romantic and absolutely irresponsible.

In the evening, when the students came back to the camp, I was feeling a little better and had actually fallen asleep beside my tent. When I opened my eyes I saw my two 'knights' standing beside me, each holding a rose in his hand. I was certainly happy to see this apparition, especially after the day of stomach ache. I thanked them both and then immediately started smelling the roses. Holding one in each hand, I found that the rose brought by the tall skinny guy wearing the hat and neckerchief was very fragrant, while the other rose had no scent at all. And so, in this perverse way, my fate was determined. The young man whose rose had no scent understood but said nothing. But later, in the evening, when all three of us went to the seashore to have a swim he suddenly threw himself furiously into the waves. I was terrified and shrieked for help; my tall admirer rushed into the waves and helped the other guy out onto the shore. He lay there on the sand and I sat down beside him and started brushing away drops of water from his face. Was it water? Or tears? I am not sure . . .

Later, back in Moscow, there was a student ball at the Bauman Higher Technical School. The same tall guy came up to me – I recognised him immediately even though he was not wearing his hat. I felt as if it was my fate that had invited me to the dance. We danced the Argentine tango. He danced very well, leading skillfully; I guess I was his equal as I always enjoyed dancing and the Argentine tango was my favourite, with its beautiful sensual holds and expressive pauses. When the music stopped playing I looked around and saw that we were the only couple dancing: all the others had left the floor to give us room. And the crowd burst into applause. That, it was to turn out, would be the best memory associated with my future husband that I would ever have. His name was Slava Samoilovich. He was the son of lieutenant-general Grigori Samoilovich, a Hero of the Soviet Union. The General was a real hero who won his award during World War Two for his part in the forced crossing of the Dnieper River.[53]

Naturally, after our triumph at the student ball Slava started courting me very persistently. He would come to our place, sit down at the table in our kitchen and I would treat him to tea and everything else that we had in the flat at that moment. Then I would sit down beside him. There were three tables in our kitchen, one for each of the three families living in the flat. Our little cupboard stood near the kitchen door, so the other two housewives always had to go round us. Slava usually did not leave until three or four in the morning and then walked through the night across Moscow to his flat where he lived with his grandmother (his father's mother). Things continued like this for about eleven months until one day one of our neighbours said to him, 'Listen, lad, we are sick and tired of you. Either you go away forever or . . . marry her!' At first Slava was taken aback, then we both burst out laughing. He said, 'Of course! I am getting married!'

Shortly afterwards his parents unexpectedly came to Moscow, to stay for a while with Slava's granny. One day they invited us over to meet them. Slava had already told them that he was going to marry me. We arrived at their flat and had sat down to tea

---

53 In November 1943 Red Army Captain Grigori Samoilovich was in command of Field Engineer Battalion 180 during the Battle of Kiev. Under heavy German fire he led his men in the successful construction of a pontoon bridge across the River Dnieper and then defused a great number of German mines. By this outstanding act of courage and personal initiative Samoilovich and his men enabled Soviet troops to storm into the city and inflict a heavy defeat on the Wehrmacht. In recognition of his outstanding bravery and leadership Samoilovich was made a Hero of the Soviet Union and given accelerated promotion.

when, all of a sudden, we heard the General say in his commander's voice, 'And where are you going to sleep?'

My romantic nature was hurt by this, as I saw it, idiotic remark. To me, this perfectly simple, worldly question seemed utterly tactless. I could not think of any better response than to burst into tears. But Slava, instead of defending me, did nothing. He could have said, 'Father, could you not be so harsh?' But he stayed silent, either unable or unwilling to protect me, even though he could see I was crying. I kept thinking, 'Lord, what am I doing? Why don't I refuse him here and now?' Perhaps I mistook our eleven month courtship for love . . . so I said nothing either.

Slava and I left together. I realised that Slava's parents, especially his mother, did not much like me. It was the first serious mistake I made in my relationship with Slava and his family. I could have said, 'If I am not good enough for you I can leave. I have enough admirers'. But . . . I left the flat without saying a word, and Slava followed me.

Some months before I first met Slava an event had taken place that shaped my attitude towards sex. I had become acquainted with a film director called Yevgeny Vassiliev.[54] I had been invited to a party by a woman who was friend of his who lived not far from the Moscow Zoo. There I met Yevgeny Vassiliev. He was talking a lot about cinema; by that time he had already made two films. I also met Yevgeny Vassiliev's wife at the party, the actress Danuta Stolyarskaya (like the lady who had invited me to the party, her family were Polish). Both the ladies, like Yevgeny, were from the cinema world – the world which interested and attracted

---

54 A minor Soviet film director who, after some initial success, later more or less disappeared. However his wife, Danuta Stolyarskaya, who at the time when Tamara first met her had only appeared in two films, went on to achieve considerable success, playing major roles in more than two dozen Soviet films. She died aged 81 in 2011.

me so much. Yevgeny took to me at once and during one of my subsequent visits to my hostess's flat asked me out on a date.

I was reckless, mischievous and was expecting . . . something. When I arrived at the flat at the appointed time I was struck by the air of mystery that surrounded my visit: I was expected to quietly take off my shoes and tip-toe to his room. I can't say that I was immoral, but I think any girl would have been swept away by the whole atmosphere of romantic intrigue that Yevgeny had created. He pressed his finger to his lips to warn me to keep silent. Holding my shoes in my hand I tip-toed past a number of closed doors . . . The room I entered was dimly lit, in gentle shadow; on the table there was a bouquet of fresh roses, a bottle of wine and a fluffy yellow teddy-bear! Naturally, I was conquered: I was expected and Yevgeny had taken great care in preparing for our meeting. He realised that, although I was twenty years old, I was still a child. I rushed to the teddy-bear and . . . to Yevgeny. In that instant he knew that his 'method' was a success. We were both smiling. We drank a little of the wine from beautiful glasses and then I stretched out my hands towards him . . . He turned on some quiet music and we danced. I was flying away, higher and higher, remembering my very first childish love for the Captain First Rank. The room seemed filled with tenderness. He kissed me softly and drew me gently to him. Enchanted by the tender caresses of my partner, I did not resist. Then I felt pain and – nothing else. There was no ecstasy, none of that delight which simultaneously uplifts both man and woman to the heavens. There was just pain. I felt something warm flowing down my legs – it was my own blood. My hymen was broken and I had become a woman! I was proud of it. I jumped like a child saying, 'That's it! Now I am a woman, I am a woman!'

Yevgeny realised that he had not made me especially happy but all the same he was touched by my childish reaction. I was not upset because of the pain I felt or because I did not experience any uplifting delight. His tenderness enfolded me like a cocoon. I took the teddy-bear in my arms and immediately fell asleep. Yevgeny sat beside me repeating, 'What a child you still are!'

In the morning we disappeared from the flat like ghosts . . . The teddy-bear came with me; it lived with me for a long time and later my son used to play with it – having no inkling that once his mother had nearly become a charmed loose woman without even knowing what sex was. All she knew was that she could charm men. She had known it since the time of the Captain First Rank from Tallinn.

After having intercourse with Yevgeny I decided, for some reason, that I was in love with him, and would be forever. I begged him to let me take him out on a date. He came and I declared, 'I love you, and that's all!'

Yevgeny embraced me tenderly and softly, as only he could, and whispered in my ear, 'My little silly girl, it was not me but the teddy-bear that enchanted you. You are still a child. The fact that I made you a woman doesn't matter. Sooner or later it would have happened anyway. And it is good that I was your first man and that you remember me so kindly. Time will pass and you will see that I am right: you will really fall in love with someone and love them with your whole heart. And as for me, I will never forget either you or the enchanted feeling of our intimacy – because one cannot forget such a charming creature as you.' That was how we parted – beautifully and tenderly. He kissed me on the forehead and left.

1959

Wedding

In spite of what had happened when we had visited his parents, I decided to marry Slava Samoilovich. My Mother supported me, saying, 'He seems to be a nice chap and I think he loves you'. Father did not like Slava, he perhaps sensed that there was something wrong in the relationship, but he did not argue: 'Daughter, you must decide for yourself . . . ' So I did. Our wedding was put off twice because I was ill and then another problem came up: Slava's parents did not want to come to the wedding. Finally, Slava's mother, Yevgenia, agreed to come.

My Mother had a wonderful dress made for me: it was pale-pink and had a wide skirt with an underskirt – which was fashionable at the time. The hem of the skirt was decorated with small artificial forget-me-nots, and a large blue flower was to be pinned to my (at that time) luxuriant hair. The low neckline was very modest. Father looked at me when I tried on my wedding dress and said, 'Daughter, you look so beautiful!' But I detected a hint of sadness in his voice.

Before dressing myself in this finery Slava and I had to go to the registry office to sign our names in the registration book for newlyweds. I was wearing my favourite pea-green summer coat with a turndown collar. At that time there were no 'wedding palaces' as they are known today. Registry offices were usually located on the ground floor of blocks of flats. One had to sign one's name, using an old-fashioned ink pen (which you first had to dip into an ink-well). After I'd signed my name I accidentally dropped the pen which made a long black mark across my nice new coat! (Later I could not get rid of the line of ink on my coat, no matter how hard I tried.) I was shocked and thought, 'A bad omen!' But I didn't say anything. Then we went home in a taxi.[55]

My mother had reserved a nice big room in what was the most luxurious restaurant in Moscow at that time: The Prague in Arbat Street.[56] It was terribly expensive but Mother had decided to splash out as this was the wedding of her beloved one and only daughter: *gold may be easily told!*[57]

Our guests included boys and girls from Gomel and Tallinn and, naturally, almost all of my Moscow classmates. Slava invited a couple of his university friends and there were a lot of relatives from both sides. Only General Samoilovich was missing. Praise the Lord, Slava's mother Yevgenia did come. When the time came for our mothers to be introduced to each other I took my Mother by the hand and led her over to Slava's mother, saying, 'Come and meet my mother . . . ' I hesitated as I was not quite sure what I should call my mother-in-law: should I use her first name plus patronymic or just call her 'mother'? I had discussed it beforehand with my Mother and she had said, 'You know, in the old days newlyweds called their parents-in-law 'Father' and 'Mother'. So I decided to do as they did 'in the good old days' and addressed her as 'mother'. My Mother held out her hand to shake

---

55 In the Soviet Union a legal marriage ceremony had to be conducted by a state official licenced to conduct weddings. This was usually followed by a large party attended by members of the bride and groom's families and friends. These parties often included a range of traditional Russian marriage rituals as well as a feast and lots of dancing.

56 The Prague Restaurant in the middle of the city has always been one of the most famous, expensive and best restaurants in Moscow. Amongst those who ate there regularly were Leo Tolstoi, Maxim Gorki and many of the great names of the Soviet period.

57 'Gold may easily be told!' is a Russian expression used when someone is trying to impress or show off to others, saying in effect: 'See what we are made of!' or 'See what we can do!'

Tamara and Slava's wedding on 26th April 1959

hands but Yevgenia cut me short, 'Am I your mother? You have a mother of your own!' Both my Mother and I were taken aback at her remark. I knew that only MY Mother had taken care of all the wedding arrangements, and then to get such an offensive response after all her efforts . . . I thought, 'My children will never have such silly weddings!'

The wedding itself was a modest affair, but it was fun. We danced to beautiful music – the dancers being mainly the young people. In accordance with tradition, the first dance was reserved for the newlyweds: Slava and me.

After the Wedding

We took a taxi back to the two-storey wooden house to which Slava had returned every night from my place. The only room was very large (by the standards of those times) with a balcony. There was a big kitchen, a spacious toilet, a gas stove and a water pump in the yard. At first we were totally happy with everything and before winter began we managed pretty well. If I wanted to call my parents I only had to run to the telephone box which was not far from the house. We both thought that our life was quite satisfactory. Our friends often came to see us and we had nice little parties for which I used to make pancakes which everyone seemed to like.

Very soon I became pregnant. I can't say that Slava was too happy at the news.

Opposite our wooden 'shack' a big block of flats was being built. Everyone who lived in our house was excited about this: we all expected to move there as soon as it was completed. But then something strange happened. One day an official with a big black briefcase came and started checking all the tenants' documents, sorting us into two categories: those who would move into the new block of flats and those who wouldn't. At that time Slava was away doing his military reserve training, so I was alone.[58] Slava and I turned out to be ineligible for the new housing even though we were married and I was expecting a baby. Worse still, I learnt that Slava had only a temporary residence permit (a temporary *propiska*)

---

58 All young men in the USSR had to do two years' military service. University students could do this as a series of shorter periods or in one two-year lump. During it most young men were posted to military bases far from their homes.

allowing him to live in our 'shack'.[59] And this was in spite of the fact that, many years before, his father had left for the front from that very house, leaving behind his old mother and his young son Slava.

After the war Slava's father had continued his successful military career, serving in different parts of the country. At one point he had studied at a military academy in Moscow, during which time he and his wife had lived in a large house reserved for high-ranking military officers. During their travels, he and his wife both somehow forgot that their son Slava lived in Moscow on only a temporary residence permit . . . And I, as his wife, was only registered there temporarily, too. So the Soviet authorities did not want to let us move into the new block of flats. It was a hard blow, especially for me.

Although I was pregnant I still had to go to work. The Sea Transport Publishing House was on the other side of the city and to get there I had to use several different kinds of public transport which, being pregnant, I found very hard. I felt completely alone, my friends seemed to have disappeared. Then, when my Father

59 *Propiska* – an official residency permit; a registration stamp in a person's internal passport certifying that a person dwells permanently at a particular address. A person without a *propiska* could not find a job, get legal medical assistance, apply for social benefits, or vote. Without a *propiska* a person was deprived of many other things as well. A *propiska* was a vital document for all Soviet citizens. The local police kept a register of people entitled to live in a district and a person's 'internal passport', an essential document and form of identity, would be stamped to show where they were entitled to live. Normally a child was issued with a *propiska* entitling them to live in the home of their parents at the time of their birth. Upon marriage a wife would be issued with a *propiska* entitling her to live in the home of her husband. It turned out that Slava Samoilovich only had a *propiska* which entitled him and his wife to live in the wooden house, which had been his father's home, on a temporary basis.

could stand it no longer, he told me to take the matter to court. I prepared all the documents to support of our case for being re-housed. But on the day when my case came up for consideration I fell ill with a fever. Nevertheless I still went to the court but, because of my illness, I hardly knew what was going on; the only thing I heard clearly was the court's decision: 'The application is declined'.

I wrote to Slava (at his military camp). I wrote to his father, who was serving in Leningrad at the time . . . No answer.

Then one day I came home from work and found all our poor belongings lying on the snow in the yard outside our house: there was a round table, two rickety chairs and some clothes tied in a bundle with a bedsheet. I started to cry and went to the telephone box to call my Father. He said, 'Leave everything there, in the snow: they need it, so let them have it. Just take something light – something you can carry in your small case and come straight to us. I forbid you to be nervous or upset! Just dry your tears, Mother and I are waiting for you!'

So it was that I again found myself living with my parents in our fifteen-square-metre room. Mother bought me a beautiful dress for expectant mothers, which I absolutely loved: it had a white collar and small pinkish-red flowers all over the fabric. I really looked nice in it. I only suffered from morning sickness during the first part of my pregnancy, while I still had to work. As a result the whole editorial board knew about my condition from the greenish colour of my face and my frequent visits to the toilet to be sick. The second stage of my pregnancy was easier.

How I Took My Final Exams at the Pedagogical Institute

At the end of any course of study at a higher education institution in the Soviet Union students had to take the so-called state (final) exams. When the time came for me to take the first of my final exams at the Pedagogical Institute I was *very* pregnant. At that time pregnant students were not allowed to take final exams because . . . I don't know why. Maybe because the teachers wanted to protect themselves from having to deal with any unwanted medical problems: the health of an expectant mother can be very unpredictable. As soon as they discovered that a student was pregnant they would advise the student to take a gap year.

I realised that after a gap year, with a baby on my hands, I was likely to find it much more difficult to pass my exams, so I did my best to conceal my pregnancy. My belly was not too big so, with suitable clothes, this was quite possible. I read up for finals as hard as I could. When I came to take the first exam the members of the examining board did not notice my condition until I got up from the desk ready to answer. I launched into my presentation at once so that the examiners would not get a chance to stop me and would have no alternative but to listen to my answer right through to the end. I got through two more exams in the same way and then my son was born. In order to pass the rest of my finals, I used to leave my baby with my mother, run to the institute and then rush home again to feed him.

17th June 1960

Childbirth: The Way It Was in the USSR

I began to feel anxious at about five in the morning and decided that it was time to go to the maternity hospital. My parents were asleep and I didn't want to wake them up. Slava was still away doing his military service. My God! What am I going to do?! There was a telephone on the wall in the corridor which all three families living in our communal flat used. I got up, went quietly to the telephone and dialled the number of the gynaecology nurse. She listened to me and told me to put on my warm clothes but not to call for a taxi (In Moscow taxis had to be booked in advance and so calling a taxi might have been too slow). Instead she told me to walk slowly to the tram stop and take the tram to Maternity Hospital No. 25 in Shabolovka Street. So, after leaving a note for my parents: 'I am off to hospital to have my baby. Don't worry! Tom.' I set off for the tram stop.

I reached the tram stop safely, but inside the tram I began to feel much worse because of the tram's jolting and shaking. I held on to the handrail and squeezed hard in order prevent myself from groaning out loud. At last the tram reached my stop. People on the tram helped me off saying, 'You must be a brave girl going there alone!' When I entered the hospital I saw a crowd of expectant mothers, each with their relatives: parents, grandparents, husbands. Suddenly it felt hard to breathe . . . There were no empty chairs so I leaned against the wall in the corner. The door of the admission ward kept opening and letting in the future mums. At last there were none left but me. I knocked on the door. A nurse looked out and asked, 'And you, girl, what do you want?' I was at a loss . . . But then the nurse looked me over and exclaimed, 'My God, now we'll have children giving birth to babies!' She grabbed me by the hand and pulled me inside saying, 'Sit here till I call you'.

I continued to sit there until I fell asleep, laying my head on my arms on the table. I was woken up by a very loud voice addressing me, 'Gosh, she is about to deliver! Go to the shower quickly and wait: they will pick you up'. I did as I was told, then put on a hospital gown and sat down at the same table again – I couldn't stand up any longer. Then, at that moment, I heard another voice: 'Who's brought her here? There aren't any vacancies. Take her to Hospital No. 10!'

They grabbed me and put me into a car which set off for another maternity hospital. At some point while all this was happening I lost my watch and the keys to our flat.

At the next hospital I was taken to a twin-bedded ward. There was nothing on the bedside table, not even a towel. I asked, 'Why?' – 'To prevent you from strangling yourself', was the answer. I was shocked.

They told me that the woman in the other bed had been in labour for more than two days . . . I was seized with panic. But later I witnessed something even more awful. Suddenly the woman began to move along the wall trying to find something to cling on to. My eyes widened with terror: I saw her baby's head between her legs! I forgot that I had to be careful myself and ran out into the empty corridor shouting, 'Help! Help quickly! She is going to deliver right now! The baby is coming out!' At last someone heard me. They rushed to our ward, wrenched the woman off the wall and put her on the trolley, swearing at her as they did so! As they were leaving the ward, one of the medical staff barked at me, 'Don't miss your own!'

The experiences of that day reduced me to a flood of tears and I curled up in my bed, trying to hide away. But very soon I felt something hot flowing down my legs . . . I shouted as loudly as I could, 'Help!' A nurse came running in and put me on the trolley, all the time swearing fiercely at me. The thought passed through my mind, 'I wonder, can they speak plain Russian, without swearing . . . ?'

They dragged me into the delivery room where there were already three other women, making me the fourth. The woman next to me screamed, 'Get me the doctor who I saw first when I came in! Otherwise I am not going to have this baby!' I couldn't help smiling to myself even though I was terribly frightened. The doctor my neighbour was calling for so insistently did come and . . . and more or less threw himself down right across her body! I was paralyzed with terror. Two women in white gowns were bustling around me and, strangely enough, they spoke very kindly to me: 'Tamara, don't worry! Everything will be fine!' Yes, it should be fine but it was useless telling me to push and to bear down: my waters had already broken while I was still in the ward. Then that same doctor came over to me and . . . flopped down on me, too. The nurses told him, 'Go easy on her: she's only a kid and, look, she is shaking all over!'

I was terrified and I kept thinking, 'Oh, I hope he doesn't kill my baby!' Then I think I lost consciousness for a while and only came to when I heard my son crying. The nurse was holding him upside down by his legs. The baby was blue and kept on crying with all his might. Then they took him away. The big clock on the wall read 8 p.m., so I consider that the moment when my son came into this world.

They moved my trolley into the corridor and put a white-enamel basin underneath it as I was still bleeding. I lay there for some time stark naked – they had not even provided me with a bed-sheet. I was cold and thirsty. A nurse passed by my trolley and heard me whimpering for water. She saw that I was freezing and covered me with a sheet but refused to give me any water: 'It is not allowed. But instead I am going to take a wet piece of gauze and moisten your lips'. I was so grateful! And, looking back, in spite of everything, I say *Thank you* from the bottom of my heart to all those who helped my son to come into this world.

When they took me back to my ward I lay looking out of the window where I saw the silhouette of the tall, brightly lit new building of the Moscow State University. It was a long time before I was able to get to sleep, as I lay looking at the University and reliving the events of the day over and over again. I was reflecting on so many things . . . That night I decided that I wanted to have another baby, a daughter, a sister to my first-born – so that he would never be lonely. 'I must have a girl', I told myself.

At last I fell asleep. I woke up when they brought me my baby to feed. I looked at him and . . . fell in love with my boy, at once and forever. And here comes another story of roses – again of *two* roses. One of my friends (not my husband) sent three roses to my hospital ward. They were put into a jar with some water. I kept looking at them and remembering the roses brought to me from the botanic garden by those two young men so long ago. I was exhausted and soon fell asleep. The next morning when my baby was brought to me to be fed I woke up and glanced at the roses . . . only two of them were still alive, the third one had faded during the night. I looked at my little son and thought, 'It must be a sign: just the two of us will live together, young man . . . ' And so it turned out.

My dear Mother sent me a lot of blackcurrants: she had been told that I had lost a lot of blood and that blackcurrants would help me to recover. I was pleased and wrote her a thank-you letter, adding that I was going to name my son Ilya (Elijah in English). My Mother replied, 'Ilya the Prophet? Why, no. Let him be Sergei'.[60] I willingly agreed. So it was that on the 17th of June, 1960, my son Sergei was born. As it turned out, he was to be my only and – because of that – very precious child.

Today is 17th June, 2011. And it was not I who wished my son many happy returns today, but he who called me from where he was away on a business trip and greeted me on his birthday. I had been feeling so utterly lonely without him that I had kept crying all day long. And then – what joy – his telephone call! I felt ashamed of my tears and rang him back to ask him to forgive me for not being the first to wish him a happy birthday. I wished him good health, good luck and the very best of everything – of everything that I can only imagine. *I love him!*

My Father's love for my Mother was the first miracle that has always remained with me. The other wonder was my own son's birth. After my parents' death my son said to me one day, 'Mummy, I will always stay at your side.' He looks very much like his grandfather, Andrei, both outwardly and inwardly, and he loves *his* wife just as deeply. I will forever thank God and my faith for him. People say that I gave birth to him three times. Probably . . . But the main thing is that he is living and can say, 'Mummy, I will always stay at your side.'

60 Sergei is a popular name in Russia because of the Orthodox Saint Sergius (1314–92), a revered spiritual leader.

Tamara, her son Sergei and her mother in the 1960s when she was working for Georgi Fedyashin at APN Novosti

To my Son

My son is my Universe,
My Golgotha,
And the shining stars.
I carry all this
Like a cross, like chains,
Like a rainbow and the heat of the fire.
I want my journey – both happy and frightening –
To last and have no end.

Slava was away doing his reserve military training throughout almost the whole of my pregnancy. He left when my body was still nice and slim and when he came back I was already feeding the baby. I think that it was then that he began to hate his own son. Slava seemed to change, so that to me he seemed like an animal who only had love for himself with just a little bit of love for me. He seemed to see his son as something/somebody who had deprived him (the husband) of me (his wife).

When Sergei was a few months old, the General himself came to see us during one of his visits to Moscow. With so many people sharing just the one small room it was stiflingly hot and he quickly became drenched in sweat. A short while later he came again and announced, 'It is impossible to live like this!' And bought a two-room flat for us in a block of flats that was being built in Rublevskoye Highway.[61]

Until the new block of flats was completed, my son Sergei and I were invited to stay in Petrozavodsk in Karelia where the General was then serving.[62] His wife gave us a lovely perambulator which I called a *cabriolet*, because it was so cozy and well sprung. Sergei and I frequently strolled in the magnificent nearby park. I dreamt of going to the Petrozavodsk Drama Theatre[63], but my baby was too young for me to be able to take him with me.

---

61 A very prestigious part of Moscow. Housing was in very short supply but Slava's father, as a senior military officer, would have been able to exert considerable influence with the city authorities to get his son, his daughter-in-law and their baby re-housed.

62 Petrozadovsk lies on the Karelian Peninsula which joins Russia to Finland, north of St Petersburg. Petrozadovsk was founded by Peter the Great in the eighteenth century and is famed for its classical architecture.

63 The Petrozadovsk Drama Theatre is a magnificent building in the classical style which looks very like the Parthenon. The theatre is famed for its musicals and ballet performances.

Time passed and when the flats on Rublevskoye Highway were completed Slava and I returned to Moscow. It was then, when we were living together in our new flat in Moscow, that it became clear that things were no longer right in our relationship. We no longer seemed to understand each other. I found it particularly hard to understand why he did not seem to love our son Sergei in the same way as I did. Worse still, Slava did not want us to have the second child that I so much wanted. In the end it was that, more than anything else, that ruined our relationship. I have loved my son since the moment of his conception and I adore him still. But his father does not seem to need him. All my efforts to interest my husband in his son failed. When I became pregnant a second time, my husband told me that I should have an abortion and I did.

In the meantime something had gone wrong in my Mother and Father's relationship. My Mother went back to Siberia to see several of her relatives who had survived Stalin's persecution. But she did not go with my Father but with another man! I disliked him from the start and made my choice immediately. I stayed with Father and said to my Mother, 'You have got someone who loves you, but Father hasn't. He only has me. Who is going to take care of him, to cook and wash for him? You have chosen another man, so I'm staying with Father.' Mother was probably not expecting me to say these things to her and she was hurt.

Father missed my Mother terribly. It caused him enormous pain: he had loved her madly since he was nineteen and was, I think, a one-woman man. In great distress, he sent her a telegram saying, 'Tamara has had both her legs cut off'. I can only imagine the kind of nightmare Mother must have lived through before she could get back to Moscow. My baby and I were visiting my friend Valeria who lived next-door. My son was asleep when all of a sudden the doorbell rang, making us jump. When Valeria opened the door I saw my Mother who immediately rushed towards me like a mad woman. She threw her arms around my legs and whispered, 'Oh, praise the Lord, they are intact!' then burst into tears. In this brutal way Father got back the woman he loved, my Mother.

After this terrible episode my parents started to have frequent quarrels. During their rows I would go into the kitchen so as not to hear. So, when the General invited me and my son to stay with him again – this time in Leningrad – I willingly agreed. When we arrived in Leningrad a young soldier picked us up in a car and drove us to a big house not far from the Smolny.[64]

Carrying little Sergei in my arms, I went up to the first floor and opened the door of the flat. I stopped dead, stunned by what I saw: the dining room was lit by a crystal chandelier, the fine furniture was made of precious wood . . . I was especially impressed by a bureau with lots of drawers, each with its own small lock. The flat had four rooms. One of them, which had been Slava's younger brother Sasha's room, was given to me and my son. Sasha turned out to be a sour person and for a long time afterwards seemed to bear a grudge because we had deprived him of his room. Unlike his older brother, to me he seemed quarrelsome, rather foolish and unkind. I tried to have as little to do with him as possible. I had my son to look after and was totally absorbed in caring for him.

The General's mother Sofia, the kindest old lady, was also staying with us. She was the only member of the Samoilovich family who always treated me with friendliness and affection. I appreciated her attitude so much!

The General was posted to Moscow to take up a position in a

64 During the 1917 Revolution the Smolny Institute for Noble Maidens had been used by Lenin as his headquarters. In 1934 Kirov was murdered in the Smolny and later it became the office of the Mayor of Leningrad – St Petersburg – and the headquarters of the local Communist Party.

military academy. His wife had been looking forward to this: she was a Muscovite by birth and wanted to go back to live in her native city. Using his name and connections, the General promised to get me a permanent registration (*propiska*) to allow me, Slava and our son to continue to live in that magnificent building in Leningrad. At first I was so happy: at last all the three of us would be living together as a family, in really high quality accommodation. I sent word to my Mother to tell her the good news. But my dream was not to come true. My parents were still not getting on well with each other. I loved them both dearly and realised that if I left them forever they would separate. I felt that I was the connecting link, the one thing that made them stay together – both of them loved me and my son. So I gave up the opportunity to live in a nice flat in Leningrad in order to keep my parents together.

We returned to the fifteen-square-metre room in the Moscow communal flat. I do not know whether my sacrifice was appreciated at the time, but later I suffered greatly because of my unselfish act.

Because my son absolutely refused to be left in a nursery – he cried and protested violently whenever we tried to leave him in one – my Mother gave up her job for three years so as to be able to look after her grandson and allow me to work. The editor-in-chief of the publishing house had called me and said, 'Tamara, if you can resume work immediately, we will make you senior editor'. My maternity leave had been unpaid. If I accepted the offer I would get not only a good salary of one-hundred-and-seventy rubles but be doing a job that I loved, with a team of people I loved. Naturally, I agreed and in April 1961, when Sergei was ten months old, I went back to work at the Sea Transport Publishing House. By that time Sergei had stopped breast-feeding, so I felt free to accept the offer.

1964

How I Came to Work at the Novosti Press Agency

As I have explained, Father now worked in the construction industry and at that time he was in charge of a major renovation of the Novosti Press Agency's head office in Pushkin Square. Now and then I used to go there to see him at work. Although I found my work at the Sea Transport Publishing House very interesting I dreamt that one day I would work for the Novosti Press Agency.[65]

65 The Novosti Press Agency's roots went back to 1941, immediately after Hitler's invasion of Russia, when the Soviet government set up the Soviet Information Bureau (*Sovinformburo*) to inform radio listeners, newspaper and magazine readers around the world, Communist resistance movements in occupied Europe and their allies against Nazism, about the struggle of the Soviet people. After the war, through a network of over one thousand newspapers, more than five hundred magazines and eighteen radio stations in twenty-three countries, plus Soviet embassies, friendship societies, trade unions and other organisations, *Sovinformburo* continued to provide information about Soviet foreign and domestic policy. In 1961, after the death of Stalin, *Sovinformburo* was reborn as the Novosti Press Agency (APN), becoming the leading press agency and information body for public organisations throughout the Soviet Union. Its aims were officially stated as being 'to contribute to mutual understanding, trust and friendship among peoples in every possible way by publishing accurate information about the USSR abroad and informing the Soviet public about the life of peoples in foreign countries'. Novosti's motto was 'Information for Peace, for Friendship of the Nations.' It had bureaux in more than two hundred countries and published newspapers, books and magazines in forty-five languages. Between 1965 and 1967 alone it is reputed to have printed no less than thirty-five million books, brochures, albums and guides in Russian and many other languages. Its headquarters were in Pushkin Square in central Moscow.

Knowing of my dream, my Father did his best to get me a job at Novosti, even though it might have to be at the lowest possible level. He believed that once I had job there I would be able to build up my career myself. So Father put my name forward for a job in what was called the Foreign Dispatch Office: actually, it was just a postal service for mailing and receiving correspondence from abroad. I knew English and so they readily agreed to hire me. However, the job was not quite what I wanted.

Unfortunately, all the staff in my department were women and nearly all of them took an instant dislike to me, sometimes mocking me cruelly. I usually went to work wearing a white blouse and a skirt with a belt. So these 'kind' ladies invented an amusement: without me noticing, they used to creep up behind me and drop an insect down the collar of my blouse. I would become frightened and struggle to reach inside to get it out. But every time it proved impossible. Then, in full view of all these women, I would have to take off my skirt to let the insect out. The insect would jump out and fly away to the accompaniment of the ladies' happy laughter and my tears. One day when they played this practical joke on me a young woman (called Alya), who was an assistant to Fedyashin, head of the Western department of the Agency, happened to be in the room. She was so shocked by what she witnessed that she told her boss about it, adding that it was necessary to move me from the Foreign Dispatch Office to a job on one of the editorial boards. Alya was pregnant and her idea was to let me stand in for her during her maternity leave. She introduced me to Fedyashin and he gave his consent. So in this way, in almost no time, I rose from the ground floor to the second floor of the Agency, by becoming an assistant to Georgi Fedyashin. He was a handsome middle-aged man who had a good knowledge of several languages, but especially French.

I worked hard, formed my own opinions about things and was not afraid to express my views, and I think I was a real help to my new boss. I never turned down any kind of job: for example, I would make tea or coffee and then serve it on a nicely laid tray to Fedyashin and his visitors. One morning, on my way to work, I tripped on the steps as I was getting on to the bus and instinctively reached out to grab something to stop myself falling down. As soon as I did so I heard a faint crackling, ripping sound: my left sleeve was tearing apart at the seam! What on earth was I to do when I got to the office? Where would I get a needle and thread? Where would I find a quiet place to undress? But when I got to the office all these questions had to be left unanswered because as soon as I arrived I was told that Fedyashin was meeting a foreign delegation in his office. I rushed downstairs to get the tray, cups, coffee, biscuits and sweets. Then, when I entered Fedyashin's office, I elegantly laid the table while all the time keeping my left arm pressed tight in to my body in such a way that nobody would notice the damage to my sleeve. Then, before leaving the room, I bowed to the guests in the Japanese manner and left without turning my back on them. Returning to my desk I said to myself, 'That was close!' From then on I always kept a needle and a range of different coloured threads in my desk.

Once Alya's maternity leave was over and she had returned to her work, Fedyashin began to think about how to find me a good position – he must have been satisfied with my work. Besides Alya said to him, 'Georgi Arsenievich[66], you really can't send her back to the Foreign Dispatch Office to be eaten alive!' Fedyashin smiled and said, 'Don't worry, girls, I won't let that happen!' He summoned the editor-in-chief of the TV news editorial board, Georgi Bolshakov, and said to him, 'Yegor, do everything you can to get Tamara a job working with you. You'll never regret it!' Bolshakov scratched his head and said, 'You know, Yegor, she used to be a senior editor in her previous job, and I only have

66 Fedyashin's forename and patronymic.

Tamara and her son later in the 1960s

vacancies for editors . . . ' Fedyashin replied, 'Don't worry. Tamara is a smart girl and I am sure you will soon make her a senior editor.'[67]

In this way I was transferred to the TV news editorial board. Father had been right to put his trust in me: I did not let him down! I thank him very, very much. And I am equally grateful to Georgi Fedyashin and Georgi Bolshakov.

67 Both Fedyashin and Bolshakov had the same first name – Georgi. In Russia people with the name Georgi are often known familiarly as Yegor and the fact that Fedyashin and Bolshakov called each other Yegor indicates that they were on friendly terms.

Commentary

As we have seen, tensions in Tamara and Slava Samoilovich's marriage had started to develop soon after the birth of their son, Sergei, and in 1964, shortly after Tamara started working at the Novosti Press Agency, they separated. They were divorced on 30th December 1964.

Observations

How difficult men's roads are!
If only girls were told about that earlier . . .
Then grown up girls
Would have taken better care of their husbands –
Like the apple of their eyes
At the threshold . . .

I am Assigned to Work with my Englishmen

In the autumn of 1966, after I had been working for Georgi
Bolshakov in Novosti's TV editorial department for a little over a
year, I was assigned to work on an international documentary co-
production project between Novosti and the British ITV company
Granada Television. It was to be a documentary account of the
1917 October Revolution, based on the book *Ten Days That
Shook the World* by John Reed, and was intended to mark the
fiftieth anniversary of the Bolshevik seizure of power. Reed was an
American journalist who had been in Petrograd (St Petersburg) in
1917 and witnessed many of the key events of the revolution.
Vladimir Ilich Lenin, the leader of the Bolsheviks and first Head of
State of the USSR, had himself written an introduction to the first
edition of Reed's book. It was through working on the film that I
came to meet the famous Russian film director Grigori
Aklexandrov,[68] his wife, the film star and actress, Lyubov Orlova,[69]

---

68 Grigori Alexandrov (1903-1983). Alexandrov started out as an actor
    and musician, playing leading parts in and co-writing the scripts for
    Sergei Eisenstein's early films *Strike* (1924) and *Battleship Potemkin*
    (1925) before going on to co-direct with Eisenstein, *October* (1928) and
    The General Line (1929). Alexandrov went on to direct a string of
    extremely popular musical comedies starring his wife Lyubov Orlova,
    Jazz Comedy (1934), *Circus* (1936) and *Volga, Volga* (1938). In 1944 he
    succeeded Eisenstein as the head of the main Soviet film studio and
    production company Mosfilm and in 1949 directed the internationally
    acclaimed *Meeting on the Elbe*.
69 Lyubov Orlova (1902-1975) singer and actress, often described as the
    first genuine Soviet movie star. Said to be Stalin's favourite film star,
    Lyuba, as she was familiarly known, was a kind of Soviet Ginger
    Rogers adored by millions.

Dmitri Shostakovich's student and friend the composer Revol Bunin[70], several survivors – by then old men – who had taken part in the events of 1917, many other interesting people and the two Englishmen who would become my friends – Norman Swallow and Michael Darlow.

70 Revol Bunin (1924–1976). In 1943 Revol Bunin was personally selected by Shostakovich to be his first composition student at the Moscow Conservatoire of Music. Later he became a co-professor with Shostakovich at the Leningrad Conservatoire. Although his father had played an active role in the 1917 Bolshevik revolution (his father named him Revol in commemoration of the revolution), unlike many other composers and creative people in the Soviet Union Revol always refused to join the Communist Party even though his career suffered as a result. When Shostakovich lost his professorship following the introduction of rigid new government regulations on music and art in the USSR, Bunin was sacked from his professorship at the Conservatoire as well. For years Bunin was forced to make his living by writing scores for other composers. In this way several of his compositions were awarded the Stalin Prize but Bunin's name was always kept a secret from the members of the selection committee and so he never received the public recognition he deserved. Some years after Stalin's death he was again able to resume his career openly. In all he composed nine symphonies, numerous concerti, an opera and many other works, plus the scores for forty-eight movies.

Commentary

How I came to meet Tamara

Ten Days that Shook the World was something of a first – in 1966 no British broadcaster had ever co-produced a major TV programme with the Russians. The contract for the programme had been negotiated at the highest level, directly between the founder and owner of Granada Television, Sidney Bernstein, and the President of Novosti's controlling Board. Contact with Novosti had been established by Bernstein himself through his long-standing friendship with the head of Mosfilm Studios in Moscow, Grigori Alexandrov, who had been the co-director, with Sergei Eisenstein, of the classic Soviet films *October* and *The General Line*.[71] Alexandrov was to be the Russian producer of the programme.

Granada's role in the co-production would be to provide a producer to work with Alexandrov, editing and post-production for the film, to carry out research and find archive film footage in the West, to supply the film stock and to buy APN Novosti a new, up-to-date, Arriflex sixteen-millimetre camera and the latest sound recording equipment. Novosti was to supply Russian archive film footage and provide camera crews, facilities, research and other assistance while we were in Russia. The film's script, based on John Reed's classic eye-

---

71 Bernstein had got to know Alexandrov in 1929 when he and Ivor Montagu had invited Eisenstein and Alexandrov to London to introduce the first British screening at the London Film Society of Eisenstein's classic, ground-breaking film *Battleship Potemkin*, which Alexandrov had helped to script and in which he had played a leading role.

witness account of the events of 1917, was to be written and agreed by Granada and Novosti jointly.

However, the project had run into trouble. Shortly after the contract was signed an experienced Granada producer had flown out to Moscow to start work on the project but returned empty-handed after Novosti had failed to provide the promised level of assistance. Following this setback Bernstein had sent one of his most trusted production managers, Gerald Valvona, to Moscow to determine whether Novosti intended to go ahead with the production or not. After a few days in Moscow Gerald Valvona was satisfied that Novosti would honour the contract and asked Bernstein to send another producer out to Moscow immediately.

The producer selected for this potentially tricky assignment was Norman Swallow, a very experienced, multi-award winning documentary and current affairs producer and director who had worked for both the BBC and ITV. As well as making a string of highly acclaimed documentaries Norman Swallow had handled a range of potentially controversial and contentious political assignments, such as Anthony Eden's Prime Ministerial television address to the nation at the height of the 1956 Suez Crisis. However, Norman had a number of other pre-existing programme commitments, so it was decided that I (then at the beginning of my career as a TV director, having been a programme researcher) would accompany Norman to Moscow and then, once a good working relationship had been achieved with Novosti, stay on to start detailed work on the project while Norman returned to London to complete his other assignments.

So on Thursday 10th November 1966, the date specifically agreed by Gerald Valvona with Novosti, Norman and I checked-in at Heathrow for the daily Aeroflot flight to Moscow. While waiting in the Departure Lounge for our flight to be called Norman decided, very wisely it later turned out, to buy a five-pack of bottles of Scotch whisky in the duty-free shop – 'I am told that the Russians like to drink,' he said. A man of unfailing good humour, ready with a joke to break the tension in any difficult situation, Norman always appeared unflappable and almost never lost his temper. He was, therefore, an ideal person to take on such a potentially contentious assignment – an assignment which, we were to come to see over the next few weeks, placed us in much the same position as two atheists assigned by their bosses to collaborate on a co-production with the Vatican about the Virgin birth!

Landing in the late afternoon at Moscow's Sheremetyevo Airport we were met by Gerald Valvona and driven to our hotel, The National, next to Red Square and opposite the Kremlin. After a first dinner of Borscht, kebabs, vodka and some wine in the hotel's stately, but crowded, gilded restaurant Norman and I took our first short evening stroll around Red Square and past Lenin's Mausoleum. The schedule for the next day, agreed by Valvona with Novosti, was that Norman and I would look around the parts of the Kremlin that were open to the public and then, in the early afternoon, have our first scheduled meeting with our Russian counterparts. However, next day when we returned to the hotel at lunchtime after our visit to the Kremlin, we were handed a message from Novosti saying that no one would be available to meet us until 4.15p.m. Later that afternoon the meeting was again postponed, this time until 9.15a.m. the next morning. So, after a quick lunch, Norman and I went to the British Embassy to register our presence in Moscow (in those days informing the British Embassy of your presence in the USSR was regarded by journalists and TV crews as a sensible precaution in case of trouble with the Soviet authorities). At the embassy we met the Cultural Attaché who, while saying that he thought things looked good for our planned co-production, cautioned us that hidden microphones would be eavesdropping on our every word in almost every place we visited in Russia and that our every word and action would be reported back to the KGB. In those days the whole business of there being hidden microphones everywhere and people following you wherever you went was a constant source of conversation and concern among Westerners visiting the Soviet Bloc countries. For Norman and me it quickly became the source of a private running joke. We invented a fictional character called Fotheringhay who followed us, holding an old copy of *The Times* upsidedown which he pretended to read, whenever we went out for a walk or took the Metro to some distant part of Moscow. What the Soviet authorities, if they were listening to us, made of these conversations I dare not think. Perhaps they thought we were mad or conversing in some elaborate code. Over time, however, we did come to have well-grounded suspicions that some specific offices and hotel rooms which we used regularly were bugged by the authorities. But we turned this to our own advantage. If a particular official was being particularly obstructive or Novosti was dragging its feet more than usual over something, Norman and I would stage a conversation in a room where we had reason to believe there were hidden microphones. We would complain to each other vehemently about whichever official was being difficult or the issue over which Novosti was dragging its feet.

If things were going particularly badly our conversation would end with us agreeing that if the problem was not sorted out by a certain time or date we would have no alternative but to return to London and advise Sidney Bernstein that the production was off. More than once this stratagem appeared to produce results. Things that we had been told were impossible suddenly became possible, an obstructive official would miraculously find himself moved to another assignment to be replaced by someone more helpful.

The following morning, Saturday, at 9.15a.m. on the dot, a Novosti car arrived at the hotel and we were driven to Novosti's Moscow headquarters. There we had a brief meeting with two relatively junior Novosti officials, during which a timetable was drawn up for the following week, and then, after promising us that someone more senior from Novosti would be in touch with us over the weekend, we were shown out. When we got back to the hotel we went to Norman's room and held the first of our staged conversations. We bemoaned the fact that in spite of having flown out to Moscow on the day and flight specifically agreed with Novosti, we had now been in the city for two full days and achieved virtually nothing. We then went on to agree that we would give Novosti exactly one week in which to demonstrate that they were in earnest about this co-production, after which, if there was still no satisfactory progress, we would return to the UK and tell Bernstein that the production was off. Until then, we said, we would be on time for every appointment, but if no one from Novosti showed up after half-an-hour of the appointed time, we would leave. We added that, if the production came to nothing, we would be unlikely ever to be in Moscow again and so while we were here we should make the best of our time in the city. We would fill the hours when we should have been working, but had been let down by our Novosti colleagues, by having a good time. We would see all the famous sights, visit the galleries and well-known buildings, go to the Bolshoi Ballet and Opera, try to get in to see a Moscow Dynamo match and so on.

Despite the promises of the two junior Novosti officials the whole weekend passed without anyone from Novosti contacting us. So, true to our word, we went out and enjoyed ourselves. We saw *Giselle* at The Bolshoi, visited the Museum of the Revolution and an art gallery, where we saw some wonderful, unfamiliar paintings by Michelangelo, Rembrandt and the French Impressionists, together with some unbelievably awful modern Soviet works. Unable to get tickets for Moscow Dynamo we went to a cinema and saw a conventional Soviet fiction film about the Revolution. Wherever we went in the city we felt completely safe, unlike in some capitals of the world, and found people unfailingly helpful and friendly. After dinner each evening we walked around Red Square in the falling snow and watched the small army of snow-ploughs and lady road-sweepers clearing it as soon as it settled. On our second evening, in the pedestrian tunnel under the street between our hotel and the square, we were accosted by an incredibly tatty man with the words 'I am a Moscow business man. I change money at good rates'. We had been repeatedly warned never, on any account, to change 'hard', Western currency for roubles if approached by someone in the street. All too often, we had been told, these 'businessmen' offering exceptionally good rates of exchange were in reality secret policemen who, if you exchanged money, would arrest you. You would then be forced to choose between a spell in prison or working for the KGB. So we firmly told the 'business man' to buzz off, which he promptly did. A little further on two more 'businessmen' accosted us, this time in German. Norman immediately interrupted their sales pitch by saying in English 'I suppose you are Moscow business men. Well, I don't have any money!' At which point they switched to trying to sell us icons. Having made it plain that we were not in the market for these either, they, too, gave up and moved on. We quickly came to realise that such encounters were a regular feature of working in the USSR.[72]

At our brief meeting at Novosti on the Saturday we had been promised that at 9.20a.m. on Monday someone would call us at the hotel to tell us where and when we were to meet Grigori Alexandrov. Accordingly, at 9a.m. on Monday we went to Norman's room and started waiting for the phone to ring. Well over an hour passed but the phone remained silent. So at 10.30a.m. Norman phoned Novosti. They informed us that Alexandrov would now be coming into Moscow at 2p.m. and that at 2.10p.m. Novosti would phone us to tell us the time and place where we were to meet him.

So, to fill in the time, we made our way to the Lenin Museum, which we had discovered was quite close by, to try

---

72 That weekend I wrote the first of a detailed series of letters home to my wife in which, day by day, I described my experiences. Although I was careful to exclude anything that might get me or people I worked with into trouble if these letters were read by the Soviet authorities, the letters form a detailed record of my time in the USSR and I have drawn on them in compiling this account.

to begin our research. However, owing to the last minute change of plan it proved impossible to get the services of a guide or interpreter, with the result that our time in the museum was of little value. Back in the hotel I went to the Intourist bureau (Intourist was the official state travel agency of the USSR. Founded by Stalin in 1929, it was reputed to be largely staffed by members of the KGB) to try to book a car with a driver and a guide for the visits we were scheduled to make later in the week. But I was brusquely informed by the girl at the desk that we were not entitled to these things, despite that fact that Granada had already paid for them in advance. The girl told me that if I wanted a car and an interpreter I must pay for them in cash – dollars or sterling. Reluctantly I agreed. However, some hours later I was informed by another Intourist girl that we were entitled to the car, driver and interpreter after all. No explanation was offered, either for the initial refusal or the change of attitude. As I commented in my letter home to my wife, 'Such are the ways of Soviet bureaucracy – both unpredictable and unfathomable.'

After lunch we again returned to Norman's room to await the promised phone call. Again over an hour passed and the phone remained silent. At 3p.m. we again phoned Novosti and were informed that Alexandrov would now be arriving in Moscow at 6p.m. At 6.15p.m. they would phone to tell us the time of the meeting. By now thoroughly despondent, we sat in the hotel all afternoon to see if anything would happen. By 6p.m., with still no further word of any kind from Novosti about any of the plans that had been made at the brief meeting on Saturday, we had become convinced that nothing would happen and that the production would be off.

But then, bang on 6.15p.m., the head of Novosti's television division, Georgi Bolshakov, and another man walked into Norman's room. As they took off their coats and hung them on pegs by the door, each pulled a bottle of vodka from a pocket. These they placed on the table and Norman and I hastily dragged up two more chairs. Norman took two bottles of whisky from the five-pack he bought at London Airport and placed them on the table beside the bottles of vodka and we all sat down. There was still no sign of Alexandrov, but our guests assured us that he would come to our hotel at 6.15p.m. the following day. Bolshakov, a charming, well-built and clearly powerful man, spoke good English. In 1962, during the Cuban missile crisis, he had been Novosti's man in Washington and in that role had acted as the main back-door means of communication during the crisis between Khrushchev, Robert Kennedy and the White House. The other man, Zodiev, spoke no English. However, he was extremely affable and full of a mostly mute bonhomie. Over an hour passed in which more than half a bottle of Scotch and a lot of the vodka was consumed amid many expressions of good-will and toasts to friendship and the success of our project. Then the four of us went downstairs to the restaurant to eat. Norman and I asked our guests to order the correct things for a proper Russian meal and over the next two hours we consumed a small bowl of caviar each, blinis, smoked salmon, crab and various kinds of fish, together with two more bottles of vodka, quantities of mineral water and a small coffee each. During the meal repeated toasts were drunk to Anglo-Russian friendship, to our work together and the success of the project – each of us draining our small glass of vodka, chased by mineral water, after each toast. The meal was crowded with comedy, jokes and good-natured misunderstandings which arose mainly from

Norman's and my inability to speak Russian and Zodiev's total ignorance of English. Then, at 10p.m. sharp, the Russians got up and left, leaving us to pay the by now substantial bill. After paying, Norman and I went for our, by now customary, walk around Red Square to review the events of the evening without being overheard.

The next morning, Tuesday, we again sit in Norman's room waiting for a promised 9.20a.m. phone call. Again the phone remains silent and again, after waiting for almost an hour, Norman phones Novosti. We are told a man is on his way to us and, rather to our surprise, ten minutes later a man, who we have not met before and who speaks not one word of English, arrives. Accompanied by an Intourist interpreter, a girl called Natasha, we return to the Lenin Museum, visit a museum in the Kremlin and then return to the hotel. There we are joined by Bolshakov and an attractive, dark-haired young woman who seems to speak no English. She, Bolshakov tells us, knows all about the archive film that we want to view. Her name is Tamara.

Together Natasha, Tamara, Norman and I drive some distance out of the centre of Moscow to meet a Soviet historian, Professor Mintz, who Bolshakov has told us is an expert on the Revolution and will help us with the script. However, when we meet Academician Mintz it quickly becomes apparent that he has never heard of us or our film. Nevertheless, he agrees to help us. Next we return to Novosti for a promised viewing of classic Soviet films about the Revolution. We are shown into a viewing theatre, take our seats and wait. And wait. And wait. Nothing. No films appear. As the afternoon drags on people keep sticking their heads around the door to assure us that the films are on their way.

But after well over an hour still nothing has appeared and we give up. Norman is due to return to London the next day and Natasha takes him across the road to buy some vodka to take home. We then return to the hotel. We have now been in Moscow for a full five days and nothing concrete has been achieved. We are deeply despondent and almost certain that the production will come to nothing.

But then, astonishingly, at just after 6p.m., while we are sitting in Norman's room gloomily sipping whisky and lamenting the waste of time, effort and money, four people walk into the room – Bolshakov, Zodiev, Tamara and Grigori Alexandrov. They take off their coats, the three men each taking a bottle of vodka from their pockets as they do so, pull up chairs and sit down beside us. Alexandrov, a genial bear of a man in his mid-sixties, quickly proves charming, expansive and, most important of all, eager to help. As the vodka and whisky start to flow, and repeated toasts are drunk to friendship and our project's success, Alexandrov tells us that he will have a lot of time to help with our film next year. He has arranged a screening for us of his own copies of all the Eisenstein films plus relevant sections from his own films. He will show us over six-thousand feet of thirty-five-millimetre archive film (running time over an hour) about the Revolution which he has amassed over the years. Tamara has to leave early but the rest of us, after polishing off the bottles of vodka and most of the remaining whisky, make our way downstairs to the hotel restaurant in search of dinner. It is now well past 8p.m. and the restaurant is full. However, a discreet word from Bolshakov into the ear of the maître d' and, as if by magic, two waiters appear with a table from a side room, set it down by a window, swiftly lay it and invite us to sit down.

Alexandrov orders dinner – caviar (as usual!), a hot crab dish, kebabs (which prove to be very tough – 'Oh, they would be fine', Bolshakov says, 'were it not for the fact that the animal was once an Olympic athlete!'), pancakes, wine, cognac for me and vodka, lots of it, for Norman and the Russians. Alexandrov leaves before we have finished (tomorrow he has a busy schedule) but the four of us sit on downing toast after toast – each one requiring that the complete glass is downed in one. As the evening progresses in a succession of jokes and expressions of good-will and friendship, exchanged in an increasingly random mix of English, together with words of Italian, German, French and lots of mimicking, impersonations, gestures and peals of laughter, everyone seems to be getting pleasantly drunk – Norman more so than the rest of us. (By this time I am keeping my hand permanently around my glass in the hope of hiding the fact that I am no longer draining it to the bottom with every toast). Then, without warning, Norman looks straight at Bolshakov, who is sitting opposite him, and good naturedly leans across the table towards him and, pointing a finger at him unsteadily, says in a slurred voice, 'Georgi! You're a crook!' Instantly the smile vanishes from Bolshakov's face and in a quiet, iron hard voice, he says, 'What did you say?' In that instant I realise, through my own haze of alcohol, that Bolshakov, despite all the vodka he has drunk, is still stone, cold sober and that this is the moment of truth. Desperately, unable to think of anything else, I say, 'It was a joke. Norman was joking.' Then looking hard at Norman, who is sitting beside me, trying to get him to see what I am trying to do, I repeat, 'It was a joke. An English joke!' And I start to go into a sort of modified children's nursery rhyme routine, similar to 'Pat-a-cake, Pat-a-cake, Baker's man!' complete with hand gestures – rather as if Norman and I are Bob Hope and Bing Crosby in one of their old 'road' movies. After a second or two Norman catches on: 'Yes. Yes. An English joke!' Whereupon, as if by mutual consent, we launch into an improvised routine, crossing arms and slapping each other's hands. 'An English joke! An English Joke', we chant, Norman adding for good measure, 'Queen Victoria, very good man!' For some moments the two Russians look mystified and exchange puzzled looks. Then Bolshakov, his face lighting up as if in recognition, says, 'Oh, English joke!' and they both laugh. 'We drink to English joke!' says Bolshakov and we all down our glasses in one.

The moment of tension has passed. But as the conversation resumes it quickly becomes obvious that Norman is now really drunk. He starts to slowly slip down in his chair until he appears to be in imminent danger of sliding right down on to the floor. Spotting the danger, Bolshakov quickly signals a waitress for the bill and then, without a word, the two Russians get up, walk round the table to behind Norman's chair and, one on each side of him, place a hand under each of his elbows and, pulling his chair slightly out from the table as they do so, gently lift him to his feet. Then, one still on each side of him, they walk Norman quietly and discreetly through the tables of diners and out through the door, leaving me to deal with the, by then rather large, bill.

By the time I get upstairs to the end of the landing where our rooms are, the two Russians are handing the old lady, who keeps the room keys and minds a hot samovar near the top of stairs, Norman's room keys and giving her strict instructions that he is on no account to be woken before

9a.m. next morning, at which time she is to take him a cup of warm, sweet tea. They then turn to me, explain that they have undressed Norman and put him to bed and, saying that they will see us in the morning, leave.

That evening was the turning point. Although there would still be hiccups, misunderstandings and frequent encounters with obstructive officials, from then on our colleagues in Novosti were unfailingly helpful. For Bolshakov and his staff Norman was 'the man with the open heart'. He had been prepared to drop his guard and get drunk with them. From then on archives, museums and places which had previously appeared closed opened their doors to us. Later, when we told people in the British Embassy about some of the places we had visited they were wide-eyed with disbelief: 'But no Westerner has been allowed to go there since before the Revolution!'

Thirty-six hours later, after we had been in Moscow for exactly a week, Norman returned to London, leaving me behind to get on with the work. For the next eight days, until I flew on to Prague to do more research, Tamara would be my constant companion and guide – not just my researcher, her official role, but my fixer and all-round trouble-shooter as we battled with the many arms of the Soviet bureaucracy and its frequently obstructive petty apparatchiks.

More than forty years later Tamara would write down her memories of our first meeting in the National Hotel . . .

My Englishmen

I was walking along a snow-white hotel corridor and suddenly saw a young man walking towards me: he was slim, thin and seemed to me resonant like a string. I thought, 'Look! He will twang if somebody touches him!' It was Michael Darlow. A few moments later Norman Swallow appeared and Michael introduced me.

Michael was so tall, elegant and charming that I said to myself, 'Take care: don't fall in love!' Within moments I knew that we would definitely be friends. Then, just as if he had read my thoughts, a few minutes later Michael felt obliged to show me a photograph of a small, dark-haired woman who was washing up in the kitchen of their house; she was wearing a light-blue blouse and washing a deep-blue tray. Very confidentially and, at the same time, shyly, Michael told me, 'Sophie's first marriage was unhappy, but when she came to me she started smiling more often.'

These words and his confiding tone showed me that there was real love between them. I was glad for Michael and thought, 'Why do such nice chaps always choose other girls . . . ?' But it was not envy; it was inner joy: 'Praise the Lord that at least somebody is lucky!'

That was how we met. And then days of hard work followed, with endless telephone calls, negotiations, interviews and, of course, filming.

We worked until we were exhausted but supported each other with jokes and humour.

To my sorrow, Norman Swallow died in 2000. But I still smile when I remember him during one of our lunches in the Novosti cafeteria. All three of us had bought milk soup, a very common dish in Russian canteens.[73] There was bread, salt, pepper and mustard on the table. I was feeling depressed after some unsuccessful negotiations, but to make me smile, Norman added mustard, salt and pepper to his milk soup and started swallowing that 'wonderful' mixture, trying to show how pleased he was. He kept saying, 'Oh, it's so tasty! It's true, it's really delicious! I really am delighted by it!' Michael and I burst out laughing. And Norman, with his absolutely childish smile, added in Russian, 'Tamara, it's all right!'

That was what my 'stand-offish' Englishmen were like! A wonder! Grown-up boys! I love them both and want everybody who reads this story to love them, too! I am proud to have been their colleague for two years.

Commentary

Some idea of what our work with Tamara was like during those early days in Russia, and the difficulties which she routinely had to cope with, can be gleaned from letters that I wrote home at the time.

It had been agreed that on the day after Norman returned to London I was go to Leningrad with Tamara on the midnight train to recce film locations, view archive material and start meeting veterans of the Revolution. Accordingly, I had gone to the Intourist Bureau in the hotel to book my train ticket. But the girl on the desk had refused me point-blank. Without so much as looking down, let alone doing

73 This was a thin, rather tasteless gruel, common in many Slav countries. To Norman and me it tasted rather like the sort of thing you might feed to veal calves or poor children in a Dickens story. At first Tamara and her colleagues had been reluctant about allowing us to eat in the Novosti canteen as they said the food wasn't good enough.

any kind of check, she had looked straight back at me and without hesitating said 'No seats!' I had tried to remonstrate with her but she had simply turned her back on me and started dealing with another customer. So I had returned to my room, phoned Bolshakov and asked for help.

The following morning – the day we were due to travel to Leningrad – Tamara, Natasha and I spent the morning viewing in the Soviet State Film Archive and then returned to the Novosti canteen for lunch. As I noted in my letter home, Tamara had appeared carrying

' . . . an English phrase book and obviously making great efforts at learning English so as to be better able to look after me – they really guard you and put themselves out for you these people, one feels most secure with their hospitality – every Englishman here remarks on it and everyone I have met here can think of no country in the world like it. Tamara must be a good potential linguist, because she is really speaking rather well today! [At that time I did not know that Tamara had studied English at school] Anyway, after the canteen lunch, she indicated 'Now in car!' [We had sent Natasha, the interpreter, home for the afternoon]. Tamara then accompanied me back to the hotel to be sure that all my travel documents were in order – despite the fact that she should have gone home to pack for the trip to Leningrad and take her little boy to her mother who is looking after him while she is away. It was just as well that she did accompany me – Intourist had got everything into a right muddle – Luckily the HQ of Intourist is next to the hotel. We both tramped round there after drawing a blank at Intourist in the hotel – Tamara arguing away in Russian with a series of women who seemed to imply that it was quite impossible for me to do anything simple like take a train to Leningrad and spend a few nights in a hotel there without about a year's warning – 'And what was all the hurry anyway?' This despite the fact that I had notified them and handed in my visa for extending as necessary thirty-six hours before and the other important fact that I had travellers cheques in pounds sterling and was prepared to pay. Anyway HQ was no good – they suggested that we try the hotel again. Back we went – this time it was better – one helpful Intourist girl. I paid over ten pounds for accommodation and was assured that all other formalities could be gone through when I got to Leningrad. A car would call to take me to the station at 11p.m. Then Tamara insisted – despite my protests at leaving her to do the remainder of the arranging on her own – that I go to my room to pack and rest. Fifteen minutes later she appeared at the door of my room – breathless – 'Mikyul! Pliss!' And she pointed purposefully at the floor in front of where she was standing in the door. Unable to gather what she intended, I said 'OK', cheerily and strolled across. In no time she was off down the passage and downstairs – 'You come – bistro, bistro. How you say? Quick?' In the Intourist section it seemed that all was not well after all. The upshot of a lot of talk and phone ringing was that I must pay in sterling at once – no waiting for Granada's money order already made thirty-six hours before in London – for the rest of my stay in Russia – seventy-five-pounds. Of course I agreed – even though I may be a bit hard put to make ends meet by the end of my stay. By the time that had been decided it was two minutes past 7p.m., so the bank – two girls behind a desk at the other end of the room – said they closed at 7p.m. So I had had it!! Ho! Ho! Considerable altercation in Russian between various Intourist girls explaining that I was leaving for Leningrad that evening and the two bank girls explaining that they were a bank and had closed! Eventually it was all done – I think I lost on the exchange rate so that everyone could get it in round figures and make it simple for themselves – but who cares, apart from Sidney Bernstein! The drama was over.

At 11p.m. Tamara arrived at the hotel with a chauffeur-driven car and we were taken to the station. There we found the train and an attendant showed us to our sleeping compartment. It had four berths but it appeared that Tamara and I were to be the only occupants. It was then that my personal alarm bells started to ring! Norman and I, like every male Western visitor to the USSR in those days, had been repeatedly warned about 'honey traps' – about Westerners who had found themselves placed in compromising situations with attractive young Russian women and, having succumbed to a young woman's obvious attractions, found themselves being blackmailed by the Soviet authorities into working for the KGB. To Norman and me these stories of men allowing themselves to be ensnared in this way had always seemed wildly exaggerated. But now here I was about to spend a seven hour overnight train journey alone in a sleeping car with an extremely attractive young Russian woman – and what was more – this attractive young woman worked for an official Soviet state agency regarded in the West as a cover for KGB. As the minutes remaining until midnight, when the train was due to depart, dragged by I made conversation with

Tamara while secretly fretting. Then, seconds before the train pulled out of the station, the compartment door opened and a Russian came in, put down his bag and claimed one of the berths. I breathed a huge, silent, sigh of relief.

For fear that my letters might be being read by the Soviet authorities I omitted any mention of my fears from my next letter home, but did describe that night's journey to Leningrad.

. . . Apparently on sleeping car trains in Russia men and women are equal, there is, of course no segregation. But this didn't lead to any problems or embarrassment, although it did demonstrate a nice kind of unspoken etiquette – in which I followed the example of the other man and so, on cue, found myself outside in the corridor with him without any verbal request, at each 'critical' moment.

The night turned out to be quite jolly – the man, who was from Leningrad, insisted that Tamara and I help him drink the bottle of Vermouth he had with him and share his tangerines and red caviar sandwiches. Great toasts to friendship, and against the bomb, against the coupled names of L.B.J. and Mao, to Bertrand Russell, etc. All conducted on my side, there being no interpreter, in my three words of Russian. We decided that the Russians and the English must always be friends – closer and closer, etc. etc. Did not sleep well on the train – swaying at a continuous, but fairly slow, speed across about four-hundred-and-fifty miles of Russia.

The difficulties that Tamara had to put with and the off-hand and inconsiderate way in which the Soviet authorities and agencies routinely treated the people who worked for them was demonstrated again later that morning. After arriving at the station in Leningrad we had taken a taxi to the hotel.

After checking in I had gone to my room to unpack and get a bit of rest before we went out to start recceing for possible filming locations. In my letter home I continued the story:

Tamara and I had arranged to have breakfast at 10a.m., then pick up our Intourist guide and start seeing the sights. I started to wash and prepare to lie down for an hour. But my phone went and on came Tamara. 'You sleep, Mikyul?' 'No', I said. 'We have breakfast nine o'clock? You like?' 'OK,' I said – I couldn't quite make this one out, but I rapidly washed and got ready to meet her for breakfast – gone was the idea of a nice rest. Tamara appeared at the door – could she leave her bag in my room? Then the penny dropped. She hadn't got a room. This is the thing about the Russians – they look after their visitors very well, but seem to mess their own people about terribly. I must say, if I thought that I could have made myself understood downstairs in the lobby I would have gone and played merry hell. I was rather concerned – but Tamara was philosophical about it. I said that we should do no sightseeing until we had found her somewhere to stay – but she wouldn't hear of it – it now seemed that she would have to tramp round the town looking for a room – no easy thing, as there are precious few hotels in Russia. But for Tamara – like all these people it seems – the visitor must come first – and themselves a bad last. However much I protested, she insisted that she would be alright and find something. We had some breakfast and then a walk through the crowded Nevsky! Fortunately, when we returned to the hotel Tamara bumped into a friend who was also staying there and she was able to share her room.

At the appointed hour the guide appeared. She turned out to be the wife of the stage director of the Leningrad Comedy Theatre and had been to London . . . . We went all too briefly round the main places of interest in about 2 hours in a car. What a city – enhanced by a clear bright sunny day. A classic-proportioned Venice! Everything broad and well-proportioned in the classic eighteenth-century style, with a few Russian Baroque overtones. The River Neva breaking the city up into almost as many islands as Venice. The Winter Palace exactly as in all the famous pictures – but with colour. A civilised place above all things. Really delightful.

During our second visit to Russia, early in 1967, Norman and I experienced another side of Soviet life, one only rarely glimpsed by most ordinary Russian citizens. Grisha Alexandrov and his wife, Lyuba, invited us to their beautiful *dacha*, about an hour's drive out of Moscow to the south-west in a heavily restricted area reserved for the country homes of the Soviet elite. I described our visit in a letter home on 28th January 1967:

. . . into the pine forests and snow – exactly as we all picture Russia. After some inquiring around, lost in a waste of trees and deep snow – imagining wolves, bears and Anna Karenina – our driver found the *dacha*. Oh how beautiful! Alexandrov lit a log fire which roared up in the corner of the room, which was all wood and plaster – really beautiful traditional stuff – a table with benches was set at one end. Then he served hot mulled wine and spices and we looked at his collection of art treasures – two original Picasso ceramic plates hanging on the wall – very good and simple in his later style . . . a number of Leger paintings and a ceramic. Then his study and balcony overlooking the forest – covered in snow, but overhung by the roof. Then Orlova's bedroom. A beautiful antique chandelier in the centre and amethyst standing chandelier lamps on the mantelshelf – all in perfect uniform style! I had thought that such things could not exist in modern Russia – really it was something! Then back downstairs for supper. They apologised that they had no servant there, only in Moscow – though they had a rather silent grandmother who seemed to do the same function (Chekhov again!)

Dinner was huge, but crowned by Alexandrov's own cooking of various kebabs and sausages. I could nothing like eat them all. We had a vintage vodka, ordinary vodka and wine with all this. Then photographs etc. Then Orlova wanted me to dance – especially the Shake – me!! But they had no suitable music, so I did a moderate Twist and other prancing about and left it at that. For a sixty-year-old Orlova is rather extraordinary really!

Then anisette and lemon meringue pie – then coffee and cognac – then Bolshakov wanted to come home. I fear he is not himself, which is a great pity poor man, he works too hard and is a great party man when normally fit. So there it all was – the real Russia I felt – at least traditional Russia as one always pictured it!

Driving back to Moscow we passed huge blocks of flats in great new estates. Tamara it seems has lived in one of these places for two years – very good she tells me. Three rooms for her and her little boy, plus her parents – two bedrooms and one living room that is.

On another occasion, in mid-summer during the White Nights, the period in June and July when the sun barely sets and the sky remains light almost all night, Norman and I were invited to the Alexandrov's *dacha* to meet a group of their friends. Early on in the evening an extremely elegant and beautifully dressed woman was shown in and introduced to everyone simply as 'the Countess Tolstoy'. Such titles had, of course, long been banished in the Soviet Union. But, it turned out, this lady was indeed a grand-daughter of the author of *War And Peace*.[74]

On another occasion Norman and I were having dinner with the Alexandrovs in their spacious flat in central Moscow. Dinner was over and we were sitting drinking in their sitting-room. Lyuba had been drinking quite heavily all evening and seemed to become increasingly sad. Suddenly, without warning, she started to talk about the 1930s, the years of Stalin's terror, and how awful those years had been. Although she had been Stalin's favourite film star and during the 1930s had frequently been a guest at Stalin's small, private drinking parties in the Kremlin, many of her closest friends became victims of Stalin's 'Terror'.[75] Indeed, it often seemed as if he

74 Lyuba was also more distantly related to Tolstoy through her mother.

75 Lyuba's first husband, Andrey Berzin, a Deputy Commissar for Agriculture, had been arrested in 1930 and 'disappeared'. Once, during a private party in the Kremlin Lyuba asked Stalin about Berzin's fate. Stalin had replied that if she wanted to see him she could, and share his fate. Many years later Berzin was diagnosed with terminal cancer and released from prison. Lyuba and Berzin's marriage had been a marriage of convenience, unlike Lyuba's marriage to Grisha which was a life-long love match.

went out of his way to persecute her friends. Others who were present that evening in Grisha and Lyuba's flat tried to shut her up, perhaps embarrassed that she should talk about such terrible things in front of foreign guests, or perhaps fearful that their conversation was being listened to and that they would get into trouble. But Lyuba would not be silenced. She described the terrible feeling of living in perpetual fear, not knowing if you would be the next to hear the policeman's knock on the door in the middle of the night and be arrested and hustled secretly off to prison, either to disappear forever or become the victim of another show trial. Lyuba described how every morning during those years she, Grisha and their closest, most trusted circle of friends would phone each other to find out which of them had 'disappeared' in the night.

During our first three months of working with the Russians Norman and I had been surprised by how relaxed they seemed about the scripting of the film. We had assumed that getting agreement on what was said in the script about the revolutionary events, the Bolsheviks and various other leaders was likely to be the subject of much discussion and, very probably, argument. Indeed, we feared that it might prove impossible to reach agreement at all and that, as a result, the film might never be completed – 'two atheists working with the Vatican on the Virgin Birth'! We were, therefore, surprised that the subject had barely been mentioned. But then, as I explained in a letter home, on 16th February 1967:

... we were told that we must see Bolshakov at 4p.m. The thing was given a great air of importance and we speculated about what it could be. Eventually a young man appeared – thin with glasses, who we were told was a 'Board Member'

– it was clear that everyone was frightened of him. He sat down and said rather intensely that he had studied our script with great care – he smoked rather nervously and Norman and I both thought 'Ay, Ay – Here we go!' He said that there were a number of points that he wanted to raise – and off he went, rather intensely. But actually we agreed with almost everything he said – he made a number of points which Alexandrov had made earlier – mainly about not over-balancing the thing by dwelling too much on the pre-revolutionary events and about making really clear the difference between the first, 'bourgeois' revolution and the second 'Socialist' revolution.[76] And that was it. We appeared to have passed the test and everyone seemed very friendly and relieved – the young man was never properly explained, but we both agreed that he seemed a powerful figure and Norman has christened him 'Dan, Dan, The Policy Man!'

Because of the possibility of my letters being read by the Soviet authorities I did not mention the most revealing bit of the conversation with 'Dan, Dan, the Policy Man'. After he had finished going through his points about the script Norman, in a move that seemed to me to be courting disaster, broached the subject which had been worrying us most, the problem of Trotsky. We had brought Trotsky into our script –

76 In the first 'Spring' ('bourgeois') revolution, in February 1917, a mass popular uprising had resulted in the overthrow of the Tsar and the installation of a Provisional Government, led by Alexander Kerensky, which was intended to rule until elections could be held. In the second ('socialist') revolution, in October 1917, Lenin and the Bolsheviks stormed the Winter Palace in St Petersburg (Petrograd, later Leningrad) and seized power from the Menseviks and the Provisional Government.

and, we feared, potentially worse in the eyes of the Russians – had not criticised him but credited him with playing a vital role in some of the most critical events of the revolution itself. 'Oh,' responded Dan, Dan, the Policy Man, 'That is alright. Your script has three mentions of Trotsky, two mentions of Stalin and one-hundred-and-sixteen mentions of Lenin. I think the balance is just right.' Such was the mind-set with which Tamara and others had to contend in their work.

Ten Days that Shook the World was successfully completed in the summer of 1967 and transmitted, as planned, with the narration spoken by Orson Welles and music by Revol Bunin, on ITV on 6th November 1967, the fiftieth anniversary of the revolution. It received mixed reviews. *The Times* described the film as 'history made manifest . . . a masterly compilation, beautifully edited, narrated by Orson Welles at his least rhetorical, and blessed with some stirring music by Revol Bunin.' On the other hand, Milton Shulman in the London *Evening Standard* said that ' . . . truth and fiction (are) so mixed up in the programme that reality is only dimly perceived' and asked 'Is this digested, over-simplified, child's eye view of events the most we can expect from TV?' The programme was re-transmitted on ITV twenty years later to mark the seventieth anniversary of the revolution, by which time Mikhail Gorbachev was bringing about massive political, social and economic change in the Soviet Union.

The roots of the second film that I made in Russia lay in an event that occurred on the second day of my first visit to Leningrad with Tamara back in November 1966. As described earlier, Tamara and I were guided around city by a lady from Intourist. Her name was Nina Khoklova. On my first morning in Leningrad, during our first guided tour of the

Tamara and Norman Swallow outside Mosfilm sound studio

Michael Darlow, Tamara and Natasha outside the Kremlin

Darlow and Swallow filming with Russian cameraman Yuri Spilny

Norman and Lyuba Orlova

Michael and Norman in the Museum of the Revolution, Moscow

Revol Bunin, his wife, Michael, Norman and Tamara

Tamara, Michael, Georgi Bolshakov, Lyudmilla Borozdina, Lyuba Orlova and Norman in Alexandrov's Moscow flat

city, I asked Nina if she had been in Leningrad during the terrible nine-hundred day siege of the city by the Germans during the Second World War. She confirmed that, although only a child, she had remained in the city throughout. During the siege almost a third of Leningrad's three million citizens had been frozen to death, died from starvation and disease, or been killed by German bombing and shelling. Yet for nine-hundred days, from September 1941, when the German army cut the last land link connecting the city to the rest of Russia, until January 1944 when the Red Army finally defeated the Wehrmacht forces encircling it, Leningrad's citizens refused to surrender. Weeks before travelling to Russia I had worked on a Granada weekly series called *All Our Yesterdays*, which used old cinema newsreels to recall events that had occurred on the same dates exactly twenty-five years earlier. So in September 1966 I had directed an edition of *All Our Yesterdays* which recalled the start of the siege of Leningrad on 8th September 1941. In this way I had learned a little of the terrible events of the siege – at that time the story of the siege, the longest in modern history, and the suffering and heroism of Leningrad's people, were largely unknown outside Russia. As a result I wanted to know more.

The following morning, Sunday, Tamara, Nina and I drove some twenty miles out of the city to see a spot where Lenin had gone into hiding during the summer of 1917. In my letter home of 21st November 1966 I described the visit and what happened next

. . . Very beautiful, flat, wooded country – all silver birch – interspersed with water. Reminded me of that BBC film about Sibelius, but in colour . . . The cold frost, and the lake frozen over and a man fishing through a small hole in the ice – and the sun low in the sky in the middle of the day – so throwing great patches of bright light interspersed with shadows, and the reeds a grey, feathery, light brown, catching the light . . . Coming back into Leningrad we suddenly stopped, without explanation, by what looked like the forbidding granite entrance to a park, with four red flags outside flying at half-mast. I asked Nina what it was – it was thronged with people – 'The memorial to the nine-hundred-thousand killed in the siege – this is where they brought most of them to be buried.' There were two little rooms crowded with people looking at a simple display of photographs – the men with their hats off, some smell of garlic and vodka, peasant-looking women weeping. We shuffled round, some people curious, some who had obviously lived through it themselves for whom it was a ritual of grief. The pages of a little girl's diary and her picture – in childish Russian, page one says: 'Today my Granny died.' Page two: 'Today my sister died.' Page three and so on until page five: 'Today my Mummy died' and on page seven: 'Now there is only me.' The little girl, called Tanya Savich, was found, but it was too late to save her! Then we went out and looked down across a vast open space, three paths leading down steps and across about four-hundred-yards to a huge statue, past simple rectangular mounds, with a granite star at the end of each and the date '1942', etc. Nina: 'There were eight thousand people buried in each of these.' She asked if I wanted to walk to the far end and I said 'Yes.' The place was crowded with slowly walking people, and some others having their photographs taken, the sound of the Dead March came quietly, but insistently from loudspeakers. About a third of the way along it was too much for me. I stopped and let the others go on to try to hide it, but I don't think I managed – I cried.

I cry again now, remembering it all these years later. And I do the same every time I remember it. It is a mixture of grief and a kind of impotent rage – similar to the feeling I frequently had in the years while I was working on documentaries about the Holocaust. My film *The Hero City: Leningrad* and the series *Cities at War* sprang directly from that visit with Nina and Tamara to the Piskariovskoye Memorial to the dead of the Blockade of Leningrad. Many years later Tamara also still remembered our visit that day to the Memorial where hundreds of thousands of Leningraders who died in the siege are buried.

Memory

People queue for different things . . . That queue was slowly moving towards non-existence, towards something that did not exist at that moment but used to . . . and would never be forgotten, like the alarm bell that tolls at the time of danger. The danger is past but the sound of the alarm bell is still here: in our ears, hearts and souls.

The queue was rustling slightly in the semi-darkness of the memorial hall at the Piskariovskoye Cemetery in Leningrad. There was no end to the queue.

People come here to pay tribute to the memory, each in his own way. Some wander among the communal graves of all those who died during the nine-hundred-day-long Leningrad siege; they know that somewhere there lies their beloved one. Others go to memorial halls displaying the documents of the great confrontation: documents often live longer than people . . .

Petersburg . . . Petrograd . . . Leningrad . . . It is a great city preserving its greatness through centuries. Here, to the Piskariovskoye cemetery, we brought a British filmmaker. He was working for British TV with the Novosti Press Agency, on a documentary *Ten Days that Shook the World*, based on John Reed's book about the Russian revolution. The cemetery, with its siege history, had nothing to do with either John Reed or the October Revolution. But I could not skip it. I felt it was my duty to show him the material things that bore witness to the great tragedy. It was necessary not just to let him admire the 'Northern Venice' in his spare time, but to touch his heart and soul. Even today very few people in the West know the truth about the 'Great Patriotic War' the Soviet Union waged against Nazism; the war against the 'brown plague' that could have conquered the world; the war that took twenty-seven million of our people's lives, their living souls and warm hearts. Through all the post-war decades we have continued to remember the horror of losing family members and the feeling of being destitute . . .

My Englishman was absorbing the atmosphere of the Mourning Hall, glancing furtively at the suffering faces of other visitors, studying the unsteady lines of Tanya Savich's diary, looking at the photos . . . photos taken by both famous and anonymous war photographers . . . documents that could not be denied.

We left the Mourning Hall and went along the rows of communal graves (if all the graves of the cemetery were put into a single line, the line would be forty-five kilometres long). Architecture, sculpture, mosaics, poetry, music, greenery: the combined effect of all those works of art made an impression even on those who had lost nobody in the war. The key-note was a line from a poem by Olga Bergholz,[77] who stayed in Leningrad during all nine-hundred days of the siege: 'Nobody is forgotten, nothing is forgotten'.

The deep silence and the tears in the eyes of my English friend, normally very reserved people, were very expressive. He said, 'Tamara, I promise to return here, to this sacred city, to make a film about the Leningrad Siege. I promise you.'

I am grateful to human memory which preserves things both terrible and great. Memory keeps its treasures in spite of all the losses, blood and horror. It works for the sake of friendship, love and peace in the world, joining generations and continents.

[77] Olga Bergholtz is a poet best known for her work on the Leningrad radio during the siege when she became a voice and symbol of the city's courage and defiance. The words of what is probably her most famous poem commemorating the dead of the Leningrad siege are carved on a granite wall behind the eternal flame:

Here lie Leningraders
Here are city-dwellers – men, women, and children

The Piskariovskoye Memorial and Olga Bergholtz

And next to them, Red Army soldiers.
They defended you, Leningrad,
The cradle of the Revolution
With all their lives
We cannot list their noble names here,
There are so many of them under the eternal protection of granite.
But know this, you who regard these stones:
No one is forgotten, nothing is forgotten.

Early 1968

My Work with My Englishman is Stopped

Without warning, after *Ten Days that Shook the World* had been completed and we had finished filming and selecting archive material for the film about the siege of Leningrad, major changes were announced in the administration of the Novosti Press Agency. For some reason my boss was replaced by another man. Unlike Georgi Bolshakov, this man was very unpleasant. One day this new editor-in-chief called me into his office and told me that I had to hand over my responsibilities for the Leningrad film to another woman: she was going to finish it. I was not only indignant, I was puzzled: my work on the film was effectively completed. I had nothing to pass over![78]

Later I found out what the matter was: it was just envy. My work on the films had gone very successfully; I enjoyed doing my job and was radiating kindness and smiles. Besides, my Englishmen were very friendly and easy-going with me which added fuel to the fire.

I left the boss's office and outside in the corridor burst into tears. Suddenly, out of nowhere, Michael came up to me. He said quietly, 'Don't worry, Tamara! Norman and I know that *The Siege of Leningrad*, like *Ten Days that Shook the World,* is your film. It is only yours. We understand everything and ask you to hold out and not to show your tears. Deal?'

78 The woman who took over from Tamara was a typical, unsmiling, Communist party apparatchik; efficient in a mechanical kind of way but, unlike Tamara, no fun to work with. Bruce Norman, the writer and researcher, who came to Russia to work with me on the Leningrad film, used to delight in teasing her, trying to get her to smile or at least loosen up a bit. But he never succeeded.

The following day Michael returned to England to do the editing of the film. A few weeks later he came back to Moscow to show the finished film at the Novosti Press Agency.

The assembly hall was full, all the staff of the Agency had been invited to see the film; there were even people sitting on window-sills. When the full-length film (sixty minutes) about the nine hundred days of suffering and heroism was over the audience remained silent. Then, as the credits began to roll and the names of the two companies that had made the film appeared – Novosti Press Agency (USSR) and Granada (UK) – the audience in the viewing theatre burst into applause! As well as the names of the director and script writer I saw a separate line, going across the whole screen, which read, 'Novosti Press Agency editor: Tamara Samoilovich'. (At that time I still lived under my husband's family name.) My British friends had kept their promise! At that moment my eyes filled with tears, but they were tears of happiness and gratitude to those British guys for their understanding and amazing solidarity. I smiled at my friends. All of us realised the importance of the moments we had just experienced. And all the people gathered in the assembly hall of the Novosti Press Agency were applauding the two Englishmen and the one Russian woman.

They say that the British are very dry people. Nothing of the kind! They (at least those whom I know) have a wonderful sense of humour, very subtle, soft and tactful. All my life I have remembered the phrase given to me as a gift by my Englishmen: 'Take it easy, but take it!' I learned from them self-control, self-respect and generosity.

My work with Michael and Norman elevated me as a human being, as an editor and, most importantly, as a woman whom they both respected and adored. It was so wonderful! Probably that is why the whole project gave me only pleasure and not one bit of disappointment. I thank the Lord, my fate, and my bosses who, believing in me, gave me two chances to work with Granada TV for two years! We became great friends and our friendship turned out to be life-long.

Our two years' work on those two brilliant films (in spite of the tragic background of both) was an excellent education in relations between people from different systems, a school of technical expertise and the highest professionalism. I am grateful to everybody who played a part in the making those films, especially the survivors of the siege of Leningrad who shared with us their feelings and thoughts about the hard times they had endured. I appreciate the efforts of all those who received us in their offices despite their own enormous workloads and the many other calls on their time. I bow my head before the magnificent creation of the Tsar, Peter the Great – Petersburg/Leningrad – for the city's heavenly beauty and the charm of the Peterhof Palace.[79] But my greatest reverence is for all the victims of the terrible siege of Leningrad, for all who sleep in the Piskariovskoye Cemetery alongside the defenders of the unbroken city on the River Neva. We remember all those who perished. The words by Olga Bergholz: 'Nobody is forgotten, nothing is forgotten' should live within the heart and soul of everyone who lives on in this beautiful land.

Both films were a success and were well received in many countries around the world. The only country where they were NOT distributed was the Soviet Union. Each film was shown only once, in the assembly hall of the Novosti Press Agency. Out of all the many millions of Soviet citizens only the few hundred who crowded into the hall for those two special preview screenings were given the opportunity to see them.

79 Peterhof is a complex of Palaces and gardens, built on the orders of Peter the Great, sometimes referred to as the 'Russian Versailles'. It lies about twenty-five miles outside the centre of St Petersburg on the shore of the Gulf of Finland.

Commentary

By the time I had finished *The Hero City: Leningrad* and screened it for the staff at Novosti early in the summer of 1968, I already had plans to return to Russia to make another TV documentary. But talking to our Russian cameraman, Yuri Spilny, during a farewell party on the night before I returned to London, he said he feared that we would never meet again. I asked him why on earth not? And added, by way of further reassurance, 'Anyway, you will soon be able to come to London. Things are changing. Look at what is happening in Czechoslovakia.' (The summer of 1968 saw the peak of the Czech leader Alexander Dubček's programme of liberalisation in his country – the so-called 'Prague Spring' and his campaign for 'Communism with a human face'.) Yuri looked at me and shook his head sadly. 'You have spent all this time in Russia and you still don't understand a thing! Soviet tanks will be in Prague within six months. You'll see, I'm right!' I did not believe him. I said that the Russian government would never risk the damage to the USSR's international reputation of such a move. But Yuri just looked at me pityingly and said that the Soviet leaders did not care about such things. Less than three months later Yuri was proved right. In August 1968 the Soviet army rolled across the border into Czechoslovakia, crushed the Prague spring and removed Dubček.[80]

80 A few years later Yuri succeeded in getting out of Russia and flew to London. However he got no further than London Airport. Because Yuri had worked for Novosti and because of Novosti's reputation in the West as a cover for the operations of the KGB, he was refused entry to Britain. Luckily he managed avoid being

When my series *Cities at War*, of which the film about the siege of Leningrad was the third and final part, was transmitted on ITV in November 1968 it received almost universal praise, especially the programme about Leningrad. It won a string of awards around the world and transformed my career. One of the awards given to *The Hero City: Leningrad* was 'The Golden Dove' for best full length TV documentary at the Documentary Film and TV Festival in Leipzig, then in East Germany, part of the Soviet Bloc. The award included a cash prize equal in value to about seven hundred pounds in East German marks, a 'soft' currency worth little or nothing in the West. I asked the festival's organisers to donate the money to an orphanage in Leningrad – as both countries were part of the Soviet Bloc their currencies were exchangeable. The authorities in Leningrad invited me to come to Leningrad to present the money to the orphanage myself. At first I refused. I had been very distressed by the Soviet invasion of Czechoslovakia, where I had many friends who had been involved in the liberalisation movement, and was reluctant to visit the USSR so soon afterwards. A few weeks after the invasion I had been sent to Czechoslovakia by Granada, ostensibly to visit a film and TV trade fair, but in reality to contact Czech journalists and programme makers involved in the struggles of 'The Prague Spring' who had, as a result, now lost their jobs. On Granada's behalf I offered them the promise of work at Granada and help with getting into Britain if they needed to flee Czechoslovakia. In the event none of them

returned to the USSR and settled for some years in Israel. Later he moved to the USA and is today a successful film producer and children's writer.

took up our offer – as they said to me 'No one will come. Our job now is to stay in Czechoslovakia and carry on the fight for a more liberal regime.'

A month or two later the Leningrad Soviet renewed its invitation to me to come to Leningrad to present the Leipzig prize money in person. This time I accepted. For some years there had been a twinning arrangement between the cities of Leningrad and Manchester (where Granada was based) and immediately after the Soviet invasion of Czechoslovakia there had been a campaign in Manchester to sever the relationship between the two cities and end such things as youth exchange visits between them. At a public meeting in Manchester I had spoken against ending the twinning agreement, arguing that the purpose of such an arrangement was to foster better under-standing between the people of the two cities by enabling them to speak freely to each other and tell the truth about subjects over which they disagreed. Happily, the campaign to terminate the twinning agreement was defeated. But now, in view of what I had said about the issue in public, it would have been inconsistent for me to reject the invitation to visit Leningrad. So, in the summer of 1969, I returned to Russia.

At Moscow Airport I was met not by Tamara but by the woman who had taken over from her. She greeted me with the words 'I know you do not like me, but I am going to be your guide and helper during this visit.' At Novosti's offices I learned that Tamara no longer worked in the TV department at all but had been moved to the Department of Photo Information. I later learned that this had been done to reduce the chances of her coming into contact with foreigners. However, as I was in Russia as 'an honoured guest', I was in a privileged position. So when I was asked if there was anyone special I wanted to meet while I was in Moscow I said that there was – Tamara. The following day she was brought to the Novosti office and shown into a room where I had been told to wait. After we had exchanged greetings I pointedly looked around the room in a way that indicated that I suspected that it was bugged and said 'It's very stuffy in here. Please can we go out for a walk and get some fresh air?' Tamara understood at once and we left the office to walk around the Moscow streets. As we walked Tamara told me briefly what had happened to her. She had fallen in love with a foreign journalist who she had been helping for Novosti and now wanted to leave Russia to marry him. This was regarded by the Soviet authorities as tantamount to treason and as a result Tamara was in disgrace. After about an hour we returned to the Novosti office and said our goodbyes. I was due to fly on to Leningrad the next day. After that last hour walking with her through the crowded summer streets of Moscow I lost touch with Tamara for almost forty years.

Two days later, in Leningrad, I was seated next to the Chairwoman of the Leningrad Soviet at a lunch given by city's Soviet to thank me for my gift of the Leipzig prize money to the orphanage. As usual on such occasions in the USSR, a succession of toasts was being drunk to such things as Anglo-Soviet friendship, world peace, and so on. Then, without warning, one of my hosts, who was a little down the table from me, raised his glass and proposed a toast 'To the youth of Leningrad and Manchester who defeated the enemies of friendship by refusing to break the ties between the young people of our two cities'. In view of what I had said at the public meeting in Manchester about the friendship between the two cities needing to be based on speaking the truth to each other, this put me in a difficult position. Would I now live up to the principles that I had advocated and speak out, or not? I had to make an instant decision. I raised my hand to signal that I wanted to say something. The chairwoman, a large and formidable woman, who already had her vodka glass in her hand, turned to me and bowed her head a little to indicate that I could speak. I started, rather hesitantly, by saying that I was sorry but I could not drink this toast as it stood. There was complete silence and looks of surprise and bafflement on the faces around the table. I then went on to explain that the campaign to break off the twinning arrangement between Manchester and Leningrad had only been defeated on the express promise that when people from our two cities visited each other we would speak the truth to one and other, even when that was difficult. Therefore, I had now to tell my friends in Leningrad that I, like thousands of other people in Britain, had deeply disapproved of the Soviet invasion of Czechoslovakia. At the same time, I added, I would understand if my friends in Leningrad wanted to tell me how strongly they disapproved of what my government was doing in Biafra or our allies, the Americans, were doing in Vietnam.[81] I continued that, on that basis, the basis of us each telling each other the truth, I would be very happy to drink the toast. Seconds, what seemed like very long seconds,

81 A brutal civil war was raging in Nigeria between the government of Nigeria and the break-away province of Biafra. The British government was deeply implicated in supplying arms and support to the Nigerian Government in their brutal suppression of the secessionists. Similarly, the Americans were intervening militarily in the war between North and South Vietnam, their forces inflicting heavy casualties on innocent civilians.

of deep silence followed as I looked from face to face to see how they would respond. Then the chairwoman turned to me and, in a low, serious voice said, 'And we will also drink to you, Mr Darlow. You are a very brave man.' I did not interpret her words simply as a compliment, I sensed in them, rightly or wrongly, an element of threat. But, without pausing, she raised her glass of vodka and downed the contents in one. And everyone else in the room followed suit. From that moment on the lunch which, beneath the bonhomie, had until then seemed somewhat strained became far more relaxed and enjoyable. Everyone was drinking, smiling and seemed much more genuinely friendly.

After returning to London I set about developing my ideas for new programmes in Russia. However, when I applied for a visa to go back to Russia to discuss them with Novosti my application was refused. I re-applied a number of times but each time my application was turned down. So I approached an official I had got to know and trust in the Soviet Embassy to seek an explanation. He suggested lunch together in a London restaurant where we believed it unlikely we would be overheard by either the KGB or the British security services. There he told me, in confidence, that my visa applications were being blocked at the highest level – by the Soviet Minister for Culture herself. He did not understand the reason for this and asked if I had any explanation. I said that I hadn't. But privately I did have something more than a suspicion as to the reason – the lunch at the Leningrad Soviet and what I had said about friendship in response to that toast. Was that why? I will never know for sure.

1968-1969

A Flat of My Own

In 1968 Father signed a contract to work in Kolyma to build bunk houses for both the builders and for prisoners. The work was well-paid, and he wanted to earn enough money to buy a flat in Moscow for me and my son. At that time the salaries in Kolyma were much higher than in other parts of the country. Besides, Father was approaching retirement age and the work in Kolyma would provide him with a decent pension: one-hundred-and-twenty roubles per month. In Moscow pensions were small while this amount was enough to provide for a comfortable living.

The Kolyma region is located in the far north-eastern area of Russia in what is commonly known as Siberia but is actually part of the Russian Far East. Under Joseph Stalin's rule Kolyma became the most notorious region for the Gulag labour camps. A million or more people may have died en route to the area or in Kolyma's string of gold mines, road construction schemes, building, lumber and construction camps between 1932 and 1954. It was Kolyma's reputation that caused Aleksandr Solzhenitsyn, the author of *The Gulag Archipelego*, to characterize it as the Gulag system's 'pole of cold and cruelty'. In the 1960s Kolyma was still a place of imprisonment and exile.[82]

82 After Stalin's death in 1953 the regime of labour camps was slowly relaxed and, although the labour camps did not cease to exist altogether, the number of prisoners held in Kolyma was greatly reduced. As a result, in the 1960s, when the Soviet authorities wanted to develop the region's rich gold, mineral and other reserves, they needed to attract many additional skilled workers to the area. So they started to offer

I praise Father for achieving his goal: he managed to earn the largest possible pension – one hundred and twenty rubles a month – and saved enough money to buy me a flat.

In the Soviet Union most city and town flats were not owned by the people who lived in them: flats belonged to the state. However, there was a small percentage of people who could afford to buy so-called 'co-operative flats'. A group of these people would set up a 'housing co-operative', which would invest money in building a new block of flats and later each member of the co-operative would become the owner of one of the flats in the new block. It was prestigious to have a 'co-operative' flat and many housing co-operatives were set up by groups of people who all worked in the same organisation.

At that time I was still working at Novosti. My contribution to buying a new flat was as follows: I volunteered to collect and do the administrative work on the papers that would enable people to buy flats in the block that was being built by Novosti. There were not enough Novosti employees who could afford to buy flats so we stuck up notices in the streets of Moscow inviting people to join us. Our appeal got a huge response and I soon had piles of documents to process and take to the local authorities.

My organising work lasted for several months. At the same time I had to continue doing my regular editorial work, often doing it at night or weekends. I was overworked but was prepared to put up with all the difficulties. As a result, my son and I moved into a one-room flat on the eighth floor in the new block in Chertanovo.[83]

Our joy was beyond description. We had almost no furniture: there was a small sofa given to us by Mother for Sergei to sleep on,

high wages to people like Tamara's father to encourage them to take jobs in the region.

83 Chertanovo: a district in the southern outer suburbs of Moscow.

and a kitchen table. But we were happy. I gratefully accepted all the gifts that my friends gave me, including even pans and spoons.

Later Father helped me to move again, this time into a two-room flat on the fifth floor of the same building. And when tragedy struck Sergei and we needed to go to Kurgan (in southern Siberia) for his treatment and rehabilitation, Father paid to cover the full cost of the new flat. If you remember, Mikhail Bulgakov wrote sarcastically in his novel *The Master and Margarita*: 'Muscovites are corrupted by the housing problem.' We were NOT corrupted by the housing problem because of the invaluable support of my parents!

Tamara in about 1969

Tamara's son Sergei with Tamara's mother in 1976

Forbidden Love (or: Outlawed Love?)

To the memory of the enchanting and most beautiful love of
Man for Woman which happens just once in a lifetime . . .

In the mid-80s, Soviet television broadcast several Russian-American televised discussions (or 'Space Bridges') between audiences in the Soviet Union and the US, carried via satellite and co-hosted by Phil Donahue and Vladimir Pozner.[84] During the Moscow-Seattle 'Space Bridge', somebody on the American side complained that in the US advertising was mostly based on sex. One of the Russian women replied unequivocally, 'In the Soviet Union there is no sex!' The audience burst into laughter. Only I did not find it funny at all . . . I recalled my married life and realised that there had been no sex in it, in spite of the fact that I was the mother of a son.

I was brought up with the notion that sex was something obscene, something to be ashamed of. Mother always avoided this sensitive topic. She lived with my Father without understanding how important sex was for the relationship between a man and a woman. From this point of view, I can say that my Mother spoilt my life. I also recalled the disgusting episode from my childhood in Baku, when a relative of mine attempted to play a 'love game'

84 The US-Soviet Space Bridge was a series of experimental international telecasts, rather like public video-conferences, in which the participants in the two countries could see and hear each other, ask questions, receive answers and hold a dialogue. In them prominent scientists, public figures and journalists discussed a range of different topics. Owing to the reluctance of many US TV companies to pay for the rights to broadcast these Space Bridges only some eight million people in the USA watched the programmes, whereas some one-hundred-and-eighty million Soviet viewers watched them.

with me. I remember how terrified I was at the sight of a stranger sitting opposite me in a near-empty Moscow underground carriage late at night, when he produced his penis, waited for my reaction and grinned contentedly when he saw my frightened eyes . . . Later I realised that I had learned about sex from life's worst examples . . . I grew up as a very shy and morbidly clean girl.

Who knows, if my husband Slava had been more susceptible to me, with my delicate mental constitution, we might have succeeded. I am not trying to blame Slava, we were just too different, both physically and psychologically. I guess he would make a more robust woman who could make love in any conditions happy, but I needed clean bed sheets, gentle caresses and a lot of kind words . . . After making love he would turn away and fall asleep, while I would run to the bathroom in disgust, take a shower and then sit down at the kitchen table to have a cup of tea and contemplate how terrible it had been again.

After I had had my son, Sergei, I became pregnant twice more – I dreamed of having a baby girl to be a companion for Sergei – but each time I had miscarried. Then, when I became pregnant for a third time the pregnancy proved very difficult – I had almost constant nausea and other problems, so I decided to have an abortion. However, the surgery was not a success and after returning home for three days I had to go back into hospital for a further six weeks.

It was while I was in that hospital that I decided that my husband and I must part and, as soon as I was allowed to go home from hospital, I packed Sergei's things into a small bag and left to return to live with my parents in the same room in the communal apartment. Pressed by my relatives ('Your child needs a father') I made two attempts to return to Slava, but – in vain. A year later we got divorced.

My former husband married again and had another son. Sergei and I lived mainly on my salary and the support we got from my amazing parents who thought the world of their only grandson.

Commentary

Although they were divorced Tamara and Slava remained in contact largely for the sake of their son. While I was working with Tamara in Moscow on the films *Ten Days that Shook the World* and *The Hero City: Leningrad* Tamara introduced me to Slava as her husband. He struck me as a very pleasant, slightly shy, reserved young man. It was only later that I learned that they were divorced. I also met her son, Sergei – a charming little boy. I remember that on two or three occasions while I was working with her Tamara seemed particularly unhappy, but she refused to tell me what was troubling her. I did not find out the cause until many years later.

A Day-Long Marriage

Back in 1966, while I was still working as a personal assistant to Fedyashin at Novosti the head of another department, a certain Yevgeny Chernov, often used to come to our office. It so happened that he took a liking to me and started to court me, often giving me flowers.

Then he invited me to spend a few days with him camping by the River Volga, near the town of Plyos.[85] I agreed. The place was fabulously beautiful. We pitched a tent high up on the bank of the Volga. He fished and I cooked what he caught: I either fried the

---

85 A small town on the banks of the Volga, known as a 'tiny Russian Switzerland' and the summer home of a noted artist, Isaak Levitan.

fish or made a fish soup. He said my cooking was excellent. One evening we were sitting on the river bank admiring the landscape and I recalled a canoe trip I had taken when I was nineteen on Lake Seliger.[86] It was a beautiful, empty place (unlike today) only visited by hikers. I had been so young and my future life had seemed to be like a wonderful book of fairy tales that I had been impatient to open . . .

Shortly before our trip Chernov had had pneumonia and, he told me, had been prescribed an antibiotic that greatly reduced a man's fertility. So, he said, there was no need for us to take contraceptive precautions. I believed him and we became lovers. However, soon after returning to Moscow I discovered that I was pregnant. Chernov seemed indifferent to the news and, as I did not want to have an abortion, I went to see to his mother in the hope of getting some moral support. An unfriendly woman opened the door, listened to what I had to say and then said coldly, 'Yevgeny is not your husband', and slammed the door shut in my face.

A little while later I met Chernov at the entrance to the Novosti Press Agency building. He mentioned that he had been offered the post of Head of the Novosti News Bureau in Yugoslavia, which at that time was a very much sought after position. 'Would you like to come with me?' he asked. 'We would have to be married to each other to go together, so I am proposing to you'. Again I agreed.

Very soon afterwards we went to the registry office to register our marriage.[87] When I went back with him to his home I saw

---

86 Regarded as one of the most beautiful lakes in Russia, situated in the hills south of the ancient city of Novgorod.

87 In Russia a wife is not legally obliged to take her husband's surname and many Russian women continue to use their family surnames after they have married. Some women choose to continue to be known by

that he had a pretty new child's table and chair; he explained that he had bought the set of furniture for his son, who was approximately the same age as my Sergei. I was stung by what he said. Chernov knew about my son, he had met him several times, so why hadn't he bought the same for him? It seemed that it had never so much as entered his head! I always assessed my men according to their attitude towards my son – that was my main criterion.

Then it suddenly occurred to me that Chernov had only proposed to me for the sake of the job in Yugoslavia, as, according to our rules, an unmarried person could not take up a position abroad. I felt disgusted. The next morning I told Chernov that I was not going to Yugoslavia. So he went alone and I got an abortion. My second marriage had lasted for just one day. Later he initiated a divorce.

Many years later Chernov found me: he came and asked my forgiveness for everything that had happened and gave me a book he had written about Serbia in which he had inscribed: 'For Tamara Samoilovich with gratitude for everything. It seems that there was more white than black. Your Yevgeny Chernov.'

There was another thing that had finally turned Slava and me into complete strangers. When my son was eight I suddenly had an opportunity to leave Russia and go to live permanently in Switzerland. I felt happy because I was sure that my son would get an excellent education there: he would know at least four foreign languages: English, French, Italian, and German. Sergei had a very good ear and I was sure that he would pick up languages easily.

their surname by an earlier marriage even after they have re-married. So Tamara continued to be known as Tamara Samoilovich after her marriage to Yevgeny Chernov. Much later, in 1977 or 1978, Tamara changed her surname back from Samoilovich to her original family name, Astafieva.

But it was impossible to get permission from the authorities for Sergei to leave without Slava's formal agreement. But he refused to give his consent, arguing that I was a bad mother. I think he wanted to hurt me, the woman who had left him. In reality the person he hurt was his son. I suppose he never understood the harm he did by his refusal. In Geneva Sergei would have led a different life. I do not know whether it would have been better or worse but it would have been different. And I know for sure that he would not have suffered all the pain, both physical and moral, that he had to endure in Moscow and later in the city of Kurgan. And he would not have become disabled at the age of nineteen.

'Switzerland my Dream'

Long ago, in 1968, in the Siberian city of Bratsk[88] I met three wonderful men from Switzerland. One was Jean Luc Nicollier – privately I called Jean-Luc a Baron: there was something extremely noble about him, both in his manners and in his unusual politeness. The second one was Roger Tanner. He was radiant and spoke only French but understood everything thanks to his attentive eyes. He was like a Parisian teenager, *gamin*, always smiling, always ready to help. The third was Henri Brandt. He was a very special person and requires a separate description. That will come later. That was my magnificent trio from Switzerland. I did not do anything special for them, I was just doing my job, trying as hard as I could to be well-organised, rational, caring, and able to arrange for my Swiss friends to meet all the people that they needed to meet. I was proud to be their friend and I am still

88 Bratsk is in southern Siberia, not far from the border with Mongolia. Tamara had been sent there by Novosti to assist a Swiss film crew who were making a documentary about life in Siberia.

proud today, even after all the long years that have passed since 1968.

All three of them were excellent cameramen, and Henri was also a film director. The shooting in Bratsk lasted for about six weeks: from late February till the middle of April. The work was not easy, especially when we had to go into the *taiga*[89] to film woodcutters. Logging is very hard work. Our film crew was shooting the loggers as they felled one tree after another. They had to be very careful to make sure that each tree, which they had cut half-way through, fell in the right direction so that it did not injure anybody.

I accompanied the film crew on their trips to the *taiga* and watched the beautiful, tall, majestic pine trees fall to the ground. Each time the woodcutters were ready to fell another tree they would shout 'Beware!' and from the look on the faces of the film crew I could see that each of them was both shocked and deeply impressed. Every time another victim tree reached the ground and raised great fountains of snow my heart shrank. It was a very impressive, even beautiful, sight but I felt such pity for each age-old pine!

At the end of the day, as the frost started to become really bitter, we were invited to have dinner with the woodcutters in their cabin where there was a hot stove. There was a wooden table with benches around it and, as if in a fairy tale, all kinds of Siberian delicacies appeared and were put on the table: soured cabbages, salted mushrooms, jacket potatoes, bread, fried meat. Of course, there was also Russian vodka – two bottles. My Swiss friends got out a huge bottle of whisky.

Naturally, everybody started with the vodka and that was really good; our Swiss guests liked it as well. The Siberians tried the

89 The name given to the huge expanse of wild, mainly coniferous, forest that stretches across a huge band of Russia from the Finnish border and the Baltic to the Pacific.

whisky but did not enjoy it . . . There were eleven people sitting round the table and the food was disappearing very quickly. I tried some vodka as well, as I had been frozen and then had some pickles, mushrooms and potatoes. It was amazing how well people sitting round the table who spoke different languages could understand each other.

Later I went and sat on a low bench near the stove and started warming my frozen hands. Looking into the fire, I noticed how my hands were glowing in the reflected light. I recalled Pukirev's painting *The Unequal Marriage*.[90] The bride, so young, is holding a candle and her fingers are glowing. I marvel at how the painter managed to achieve that glow. In 1968 I was thirty, my fingers were beautiful and, like the girl's in the painting, were gleaming in the stove's light. Henri came and sat down beside me on the bench and we talked quietly about my Siberia and its people: strong, friendly, and generous, and about gorgeous and fearless Siberian women.

Henri turned out to be an excellent cameraman who was always ready to start shooting. This proved to be especially important when we visited the Bratsk Timber Processing Mill: we had to be particularly careful when we filmed huge logs sliding, like matchsticks, down a kind of gutter carried by a powerful stream of water. It was a breath-taking sight, especially as the logs were guided by women with heavy pole hooks, wearing quilted jackets, thick pants and, of course, head-scarves. The women were smiling,

90 Vasily Pukirev (1832–1890) was a painter whose best known painting is *The Unequal Marriage* (1862) which depicts the wedding of an elderly, high-ranking official and a young, visibly unhappy girl. The work reflects the widespread desire among Russians in the mid-nineteenth century for social reform, intending to highlight both the unequal position of women in Russian society and the widespread corruption among the ruling bureaucratic elite. Housed in the Tretyakov Gallery in Moscow, it is available on Google images.

cheering each other on and shouting out commands. My Swiss friends were so impressed that they nearly fell into the gutter themselves . . . They had never seen anything like it . . .

One day, after we had been filming in the *taiga* for a few days we were on the bus on our way back to Bratsk. Suddenly, we were spellbound by a dazzling sight: in the middle of the white snow-covered field, a pine-tree stump was burning, sparks were flying all around, making the whole scene appear both beautiful and mysterious. It offered an opportunity for some really spectacular shots! All the members of the crew were glued to the windows of the bus, sitting spellbound in admiration. Then they asked our driver to stop the bus for a few minutes so that they could take pictures. But then my mind went blank: I remembered my boss's instructions – to prevent the crew from filming anything unusual or unexplainable . . . So I blocked the exit from the bus for the cameramen, who were now all set up ready to shoot, and said in a stern voice, 'No' and folded my arms across my chest. All three of them quietly obeyed me and returned to their seats. A deathly silence fell. Nobody was looking at me or spoke to me . . . Even the driver, who had never taken part in our discussions, glanced at me, smiling ironically. The bus remained at a halt; the crew sitting in sullen silence. The huge tree stump continued to burn. Imagine the picture: night, white snow, the burning tree stump and swarms of sparks. Then I suddenly came to myself and realised how stupid I had been and immediately allowed them to start taking photographs. Thank God, they succeeded in taking some wonderful photographs of that fabulous sight!

Back on the bus, we made peace with each other. I apologised to my dear Swiss guests for my silliness and explained my behaviour. They quickly forgave me and we spent the rest of our time on the bus talking and laughing happily. Later when I recalled the episode with the burning stump, I thought: it was just a very beautiful sight but I saw in it something supernatural which, for some reason, was not supposed to be filmed by foreigners . . . God saved me from shame just in time!

When we returned to Bratsk I arranged to film in a kindergarten. We arrived at the kindergarten early in order to set up the filming equipment and then waited for the children to arrive. While we waited Henri sat down at the piano and to entertain us started playing a beautiful melody. Long before, in my youth, I had dreamed of learning to play the piano and so I sat listening to Henri with special feeling. A man playing the piano seemed incomparable to me. Besides, the heavenly melody sounded like a sign heralding something extraordinary. Suddenly I thought that the piece of music seemed like a declaration of love. The idea pierced my mind and soul, like a bolt of lightning. Our meeting was inevitable, and it did happen.

Late that night somebody knocked at my hotel room door. I was not yet asleep but was listening to the radio. I went to the door and opened it. It was Henri and he asked for permission to come in. We listened to music together for some time and then Henri said that he had never met a woman like me. I sat quietly recalling his musical declaration of love earlier in the day.

Love does not pay any attention to the marital status of a person: it does not matter whether you are single, married, or divorced. You are swept up in its mighty power and fall into Love's embrace. That was exactly what happened to us. We clung to each other and realised that no external force could separate us. We were in the wooden hotel surrounded by snow. Out of the window we could see pine-trees swaying and rustling on the bank of the Angara River.[91] I kept saying to myself, 'I did it contrary to reason but I have never felt sorry about that . . . ' It was a line from a Russian romance.

91 One of the great rivers of Russia. It flows over one thousand miles northwards from its source in Lake Baikal to join the River Yenisei which continues north to flow into the Arctic Ocean.

He quietly undressed me, tenderly kissing and caressing me as nobody had ever done before in my life. He admired my whole self, my body, every curve of my arms and legs. I saw that he was ready to die, to dissolve himself inside me because of the love he felt. I certainly answered him with admiration and delight, without considering that somewhere, far away, he had a wife and two boys. Under his enchanted gaze, I forgot about everything. I heard him saying some words in English which I did not really understand but, at the same time, I understood everything completely! It was the flowing together of two hearts, two beautiful bodies, two volcanoes . . .

I had felt from the beginning that all the three Swiss guys were in love with me, but Henri had the upper hand – he turned out to be the bravest!

We returned to Moscow, and on the following day the telephone rang in our editorial office. They were calling from the reception area of the Novosti building: 'There is a delegation from Switzerland here, will you please come down and meet them!' I ran down the central staircase and then led my three Swiss friends upstairs to our office. I was wearing a slim-fit sea-green suit and low-heeled brown suede boots; on the left lapel of the jacket there was a nice modest matching brooch. My outfit must have surprised Henri because, as we were climbing the stairs, he asked me quietly, 'Who taught you such perfect dress sense?' In Bratsk I had worn a black skirt and a black knitted jacket with a knitted collar (made by myself!), and black boots; I also had a pretty, short black-and-white checked coat. I think that the outfit I had worn in Bratsk had also been stylish and becoming and that my foreign friends must have been surprised to meet someone who could represent Russia properly in the 'fashion contest' between East and West.

In the office I introduced my three Swiss friends to everyone and told them all about our trip. Almost everyone in the office noticed Henri's infatuation with me and my high spirits. Nobody

Tamara with Brandt

knew for sure what had happened between us but it was clear that something had: he kept his eyes fixed on her, and she was just glowing inside.

As you can see, my love story with Henri Brandt was a great contrast to all my previous experiences of love and sex. It was a miracle.

A Visit to Lyudmila Borozdina

Lyudmila Borozdina was Georgi Bolshakov's first assistant. She was a very intelligent and well-educated woman with an excellent command of English. She invited Henri and me to visit her at home. I knew that she was very kindly disposed towards me, but, even so, her invitation was totally unexpected.

We arrived at her home at the appointed time and she introduced us to her husband Boris Zhutovsky, an artist.[92] The table had already been laid and we felt totally at ease, talking and helping ourselves to the light dinner. For the first time in my life I tasted vodka mixed with juice (two-thirds juice and one-third of vodka). The drink seemed both tasty and not too strong: it did not affect the drinker's mind but did help one to relax and made the conversation flow more easily.

Henri talked a lot about his travels and his book, *Nomades du Soleil,* published in 1956, devoted to his trip photographing and filming in Africa. [93] (Later he made me a gift of a very fine edition

92 Zhutovski, born in 1932, was one of the so-called 'Non-Conformist' group of Russian artists who exhibited works which did not conform to the strict norms laid down by the Party for works of art. He was one of the artists whose work was included in a famous, or notorious, exhibition in Moscow in 1962 which was visited by the Soviet leader Nikita Khrushchev. Krushchev denounced the works as 'degenerate' and got into a widely reported altercation with the leader of the group about the function of art in society. Later, however, after Khrushchev's death, his family asked the leader of the group to design the monument for Khrushchev's tombstone.

93 Henri Brandt (1921–1989) was ethnographic film maker, photographer and writer. Between 1953 and 1956, using a 16mm film camera, he made a pioneering film, *Nomades du Soliel*, about the nomadic people of Niger. This became a classic of Swiss documentary cinema. He also

of the book). Then suddenly, out of the blue, Lyudmila said to Henri, 'Take Tamara away from here as soon as possible, otherwise they will eat her up. They won't let her live and work in peace.' In response Henri shared his plans with Lyudmila: as soon as he completed his project in the Soviet Union, he intended to get divorced and immediately marry Tamara. None of us, sitting round the table that evening, could guess that my dear Lyudmila would very soon die in a car accident and this was to be my last meeting with her.

Even before his divorce from his wife was finalised (they had been separated for several years by that time), Henri tried to bring me to Switzerland by getting his friends to issue me with an invitation. But, as I have explained, my former husband, Slava Samoilovich, was unwilling to give his consent to me taking our son Sergei abroad with me. Sergei was then only seven years old. I consulted the Foreign Legal Collegium (*Inyurkollegiya*)[94] and they suggested an alternative option: I could wait till Sergei turned 10 and then bring a suit against my former husband. But I immediately visualised what would happen when the case came to court. My son would be asked, 'Who do you want to stay with, your father or your mother?' I pictured my child's frightened eyes as he struggled, unable to find the right answer and terrified at the mere thought of it. I knew that I could leave for Switzerland and leave Sergei with my parents, but I was sure that if I did so Slava would take the boy away from them. I also realised how hard it would have been for Sergei to live with his father who, I

---

wrote a book of the same title containing many excellent photographs.

94 *Inyurkollegiya* – Soviet legal aid organisation which specialised in providing Soviet citizens with legal advice on issues involving foreign law and civil disputes, such as Tamara's dispute with her husband over taking their son to live in a foreign country.

continued to believe, did not love him. I feared that if I were to leave him Sergei might suffer serious psychological harm . . . so I stayed in the Soviet Union.

I continued working at the Novosti Press Agency. In August 1968 I was sent to Novosibirsk Science Campus, famous all over the USSR as the home of all the most respected Soviet scientists.[95] My brief was to meet the scientists, to make a list of those who we wanted to interview for our documentary and to get their preliminary consent. Everything in Novosibirsk was so interesting! The scientists turned out to be a lively and comprehensively educated group of people, who thought freely and independently.

One day, in one of the campus laboratories, I overheard the news on the radio which was reporting that Soviet troops had invaded Czechoslovakia and entered Prague. I already knew about the protests there had been in Czechoslovakia against Soviet rule, but I was shocked at the news. The first thing I thought was, 'This is the end! Our 'empire' is going to pull the plug; all contacts with foreigners will again be considered a crime . . . ' What about Henri and his and my future? I felt really scared.

Having finished my work in Novosibirsk, I came back to Moscow with just one thought: 'What is going to happen now?' In our editorial office all the desks were covered with TASS reports of the world-wide public reaction to the crazy move by the USSR. Even such staunch friends of the Soviet Union as Yves Montand and Simone Signoret, adored by Soviet audiences, publicly cancelled their planned visit to the International Film

---

95 Novisibirsk in southern Siberia, some two-thousand miles east of Moscow. The science campus was established in the late 1950s by leading Soviet scientists, with the support of the Soviet authorities, to bring together leading scientists from a range of the sciences to create a centre of excellence to serve the whole of the USSR.

Festival in Moscow. In this way our Soviet leaders overnight struck another blow to the country's reputation and their own people.

I had a premonition that our wonderful love would be ruined. But still . . . hope springs eternal . . .

At the end of December, 1968, the telephone rang in our Moscow flat. From the tone of the ring I knew immediately that it was a trunk call. I picked up the receiver. A telephone operator from Geneva asked for Tamara Samoilovich and then kept telling me, '*Ne quittez pas!*' Excited, I was waiting for Henri to start talking. At last there came Henri's long-awaited voice: 'I am coming to Moscow on 30th December. I will be waiting for you at the seventh column of the Bolshoi Theatre at 7p.m.' Then I heard an awful lot of wonderful and tender words. He was speaking English. My mother and my son hardly breathed during our conversation. When I put down the receiver and told them what he had said my little son hopped and jumped and cried out 'Hooray!' and then explained to my mother, 'You know, Granny, Mother's Henri is coming!'

On the 30th, at 7p.m. sharp, I was at the entrance to the Bolshoi Theatre. The Bolshoi was one of the few places in Moscow familiar to Henri, that's why he chose it as the meeting place. Performances at Bolshoi started at seven, so there was a crowd of people waiting close to the columns. I was jumping from step to step to keep myself warm and, suddenly, I saw his arms thrown open towards me, ready to embrace me. I flopped into those arms. We were laughing and our laughter sounded completely happy. It was impossible to find a taxi on that evening, so we ran and caught a trolleybus, then changed for the bus that took us home. Mother and Sergei met us at the door (my Father was in Kolyma earning the money for his decent retirement pension). The Christmas tree was set up in the room, the flat was filled with the delicious smell of Mother's pies. The atmosphere was full of joy, warmth and comfort. We sent Father a telegram to tell him that Henri had arrived and wishing him a happy New Year. Then we sat down to have a meal of Mother's pies.

Henri had booked a room at the National Hotel, but, of course, he stayed with us. The next day we went together to the National; he took me to his room and started getting out one gift after another. He had brought toy cars for my son, a headscarf for my mother, and a music box for me. I sat down on the bed, with my eyes fixed on the box: it looked and sounded so beautiful! I got another present, too: it was a key-chain, which also had music inside it. The delightful music it played was Lara's melody from the film *Doctor Zhivago*. I still keep these precious gifts as souvenirs of that fabulous New Year celebration.

Throughout 1968 and 1969 I received letters from Henri every week; the letters were wonderful, tender and sweet. He also used to send me recordings of him playing the piano. He chose my favourite melodies and played beautifully . . .

1969

While I was working at my desk at Novosti one day I took an internal phone call: I was asked to come to the Personnel Department. I had no idea what they might want. When I entered the office and approached the desk the Head of Personnel waved a sheet of paper in front of me, right up close to my face, and asked if I knew what it was. I said I could not read it while it was so close to my eyes. I only saw that it was a letter in a foreign language and that my name appeared many times in the text. The Head of Personnel started shouting at me, calling me all kinds of dirty names. It appeared the letter was from Henri's wife (from whom he was, at that time, separated but not divorced). She wrote that my affair with Henri was an infringement on her family life, she accused me of intruding into her family and being immoral. She reminded the reader that Henri was the father of two sons and demanded that I should be punished. I do not know how she had learnt about Henri and me.

I expected to be fired immediately, as, according to unwritten Soviet rules and standards, I had committed 'a terrible crime' by having had a love affair with a foreigner. However, they only transferred me to another department within Novosti.

Commentary

Now regarded by her bosses as 'unreliable', Tamara was transferred to Novosti's Department of Photo Information where her work was less likely to bring her into contact with foreigners. My last meeting with Tamara, early in 1969, when we walked around the streets of Moscow so that our conversation would not be overheard, was shortly after this.

In the summer of 1969 Henri took a holiday and came to the Soviet Union to spend it with me. He set off in his Citroën, crossed several European countries and, finally, arrived in Odessa where I was already waiting for him.[96] We made a marvelous sea voyage from Odessa to Sochi (his car came with us on the ship).[97] In Sochi he rented a room at a hotel, as all foreigners were supposed to do, and I rented a small flat. Naturally, we did not use the hotel room at all but lived in the flat that I had rented. However, the Citroën in the yard attracted the attention of our landlady and her husband, so once, in the middle of the night, we were woken

---

96 Port city on the North West coast of the Black Sea.
97 Famous resort town on the east coast of the Black Sea.

up by the police! Foreign cars were uncommon in Russia and immediately caused suspicion: the owner of the car must be a spy, and a woman who had a love affair with a foreigner was something like a traitor to her Motherland.

I was taken to the police station and Henri was taken to the Home Office Visa Department; we both had to give a written explanation: who we were, where from, why we were together, how we had got acquainted, etc. Each of us was to write his/her own explanation independently. Later it turned out that we had written the same thing: we were tied by love, just love . . . Eventually, the policemen let us go. Henri was deeply shocked, close to a nervous breakdown: he was in love with Russia and was sure that the whole country was as hospitable as Siberia. I was shocked at the sight of his tears.

I nursed him as well as I could. The next day I got dressed in my best ready to go the police again. Henri asked me why I was wearing my most beautiful dress to meet a police officer and I explained, 'The worse, the better', which meant: the worse the situation was the better I should look!

That day I visited (separately) both the head of the Sochi police and the head of the Visa Department. I asked them the same question: 'Do you see anything wrong in true love between a man and woman?' Both answered in the negative. Then I asked them to read the explanations we had written the day before. They did. Finally, I asked, or rather ordered them to tear up both documents. Surprisingly, they did! You are not going to believe me but at the end of the conversation each of them apologised and asked me to render his apologies to Henri!

Henri was sitting on a bench on the embankment waiting for me. He hugged me and said, 'I am proud of you, my beloved, my little Tamara!' We got into his Citroën and went to a nice little restaurant to celebrate our joint victory. The restaurant was designed in rural style, with big solid wooden tables and benches, with a fence around it made of withes. We ordered some wine and something light to eat. A young couple asked our permission to sit down at the same table. The first question they asked Henri was 'Is this lady your wife?' Henri replied without hesitation, 'Yes, of course, and I love her very much!'

After lunch we went down to the sea. Henri switched on his portable tape recorder and we heard the enchanting sounds of his favourite *Concierto de Aranjuez*.[98] I came to love this melody, too. Unfortunately, they broadcast it very seldom on our radio.

It was our last day together: in the evening Henri drove me to the airport to see me off to Moscow. Strangely, they let him accompany me to the plane even though it was against the rules. He was even allowed to come with me up the first few steps of the boarding ramp. He could not stand it any longer and I saw tears rolling down his cheeks. I did my best not to burst out crying. The flight attendant was silently watching us. In spite of all our dreams and the naïve belief that we would be together and get married, we both felt deep inside that we were not going to see each other again.

That was the last time I saw him. Several months passed and a common acquaintance told me that Henri had got married. I did not believe her and wrote to Jean-Luc asking him to find Henri and get him to write me a personal letter confirming this (to me terrible) news.

Late in 1971 I got a letter from Henri saying that he had really got married and that he loved his new French wife. I did believe in his marriage but I could not make myself believe that he truly loved another woman.

In 1972 I accepted a proposal from Alexander Litkens who asked me to be his wife. I am grateful to Alexander, but it's a different story.

---

98 Concerto for orchestra and classical guitar, the best known work of the Spanish composer Joaquin Rodrigo (1901–1999).

I will be sorry until the end of my days that I did not dare to have a baby by Henri. I was only thirty-one and the baby would have been born in 1970, to be a friend for my Sergei who was dreaming of having a little brother or sister. But, instead, I was taking those Swiss contraceptive pills . . . Stupid.[99]

Perhaps Henri was the first to realise that we were not destined to be together. My country, the 'superpower', never encouraged a true and deep love if that love was born 'illegally'.

Henri died aged seventy-seven. I am grateful to that French woman who took care of him until the very end, who helped him to remain capable of the creative work that made up a major part of his life – actually work was the main thing in his life.

I trusted Henri with all my heart, I believed in him. He treated me with reverence and admiration, he greatly valued those qualities in me which were unvalued by others: my intelligence, tact, taste, sensitivity. He always said, 'Tamara is too sensitive'. That's probably why I chose him and dreamt of becoming his wife.

I believe, I know, that after one lover dies his love stays with the other one, that is – with me. I will never forget his loving words addressed to me: 'I am proud of you, my wonderful lady, my Tamara, my only woman'. Yes, my Love, and I am proud of you and of your love and care for me. My difficult love, my Henri. I do not consider your new marriage a betrayal: I think it was dictated by the instinct for self-preservation. You were gifted, talented both in love and in work, and for you work meant as much as love.

99 At that time the use of contraceptive pills in the USSR was extremely rare if not unknown. Russians practiced contraception by more traditional means – vaginal douches, condoms, withdrawal and the rhythm method. Abortion was also common. So it seems probable that Henri had deliberately brought contraceptive pills with him to Russia, perhaps in the hope of sparing Tamara the trauma of another miscarriage or termination.

Henri Brandt

It was real happiness to love such a talented man and tender lover, and I will not compare Henri to any of the men before or after him! When I look at the sky I know that you are somewhere there and one day our souls will be together and, having recalled everything and having cried over our earthly lives, they will rejoice in the beauty of that love. I believe!

The soul of a woman is beyond understanding. After I learned that Henri had got married I never ceased to love him. I have loved him for over forty years. He was always in my thoughts; I used to talk to him silently. This love warmed my heart and helped me survive.

At the same time, I lived my ordinary life. I married again and then got divorced. I worked and took care of my son and my parents. I did all the routine things that I had to; I met new people and always tried to be especially attentive and caring. It was as if I had been living two lives simultaneously. I am sure that love, even an unaccomplished one – like mine – gives a person a lot, enriches one's heart, mind and soul. I believe that, in the long run, I became stronger and better thanks to my love for Henri.

Henri

Henri Brandt (1921–1998)

My Siberian happiness,
Short as a sigh.
A tender Geneva smile.
Olives of the eyes – so delightful!

Over our thirty years of separation
How many meetings did we have?
One, two, three . . .
And then – quiet thoughts
And personal tragedies . . .
And tears in oblivion
Like strange dreams.

Then – suddenly – news of the death
Of the tender Geneva smile
And of the wonderful eyes covered now
                     with dead eyelashes
Bearing along with them to eternity
That boundless and bright dream
And the snowy image of my dear Siberia.

My Second Husband – Alexander Litkens

It was 1975 and my friend Masha, who lived in the centre of Moscow, had invited me to her birthday party. Among the guests at the party were two people I had not met before: an actor called Mark Geichman and a stage director named Alexander Litkens. As usual at parties, being a good dancer and enjoying it, I danced a lot. Evidently my dancing caught Alexander's eye and impressed him as during the evening he invited me to dance with him several times. Mark seemed impressed as well and went out of his way to compliment me. When the party ended, in the small hours of the morning, Mark invited Alexander and me to continue the party back at his place. By that time the Moscow Underground had closed down for the night and so we walked through the quiet Moscow streets to Mark's flat. By the time we got there I had developed a headache. I mentioned it to Mark and he said 'I'll give you something that will help you' and gave me a drink. It turned out to be an alcoholic spirit which I had never tried before. But, strangely, it did seem to ease the pain. Throughout the night, as we sat talking, Alexander remained permanently at my side. Then, at 5.30a.m., when the Moscow Underground re-opened, Alexander said he would accompany me home. He did, and that was the beginning of our romance.

Alexander's ancestors had come to Russia from the Baltics and, maybe, from Scotland. He believed he was descended from that proud and noble people, the Vikings. He was a gifted and out-standing person: he loved poetry and had an amazing memory – he knew lots of poems by heart and also wrote poetry himself. He was also a connoisseur of classical music and owned a large collection of records. He had graduated from a theatre school, acted in a couple of films and then become a stage director at the

Moscow Youth Theatre. Alexander was very proud of his grandfather, Yevgraf Litkens, who had been a Bolshevik and a member of the Lenin's first Bolshevik government.[100] There is a photograph of one of that Government's meetings in which he can be seen on the right of Lenin. Yevgraf Litkens had married and had a son, Sergei, who when he was a little boy quite often spent time with Nadezhda Krupskaya (Lenin's wife) or Maria Ulyanova (Lenin's sister). Yevgraf Litkens died in 1922, at the age of thirty-four: he was killed in the street by armed robbers while he was on holiday in the Crimea. In the Crimean town of Yalta there is a street named after him. Many years later, when I took my son Sergei to Yalta to recover after a series of major operations, he took a picture of me in that very street.

The life of Yevgraf Litkens's son was no less dramatic. Having completed his secondary education he entered a KGB school, from which he graduated with honours. He went on to become a KGB officer and later became involved in a notorious case.[101] He married a colleague who soon gave birth to a son, Alexander (Sasha), my future second husband. Sasha's sister used to say to me, 'You know, Sasha never loved any of his previous women as much as he loves you'.

Sasha was eight years younger than me. He was a charming and insistent admirer who, from the very first night of our courtship was always at my side, never leaving me. A few weeks later we went to visit Masha again. I was sitting in a chair and Sasha was sitting next to me with his arms around me and part of the chair as well, in a way that must have looked very comic. Masha smiled

---

100 After the 1917 Bolshevik Revolution Yevgraf Litkens played a major role in establishing the new Soviet Ministry of Education and the Arts, Narkompros, which was charged with the task of banishing illiteracy.

101 The KGB was the main security agency of the USSR. It grew from the Cheka, created in 1917 immediately after the revolution, to combat attempts at counter-revolution.

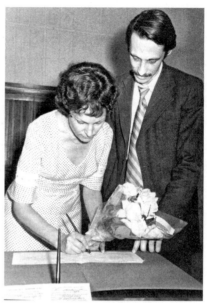

Alexander Litkens

*Tamara's marriage to
Alexander Litkens*

and said to him, 'Sasha, you love Tamara very much, don't you?'
And he replied, 'Yes, *very* much!' He was a very nice, noble, easy
going person and I felt good with him.

When he proposed I decided to consult my fourteen year old
son. He answered, 'Marry him, Mum, we will have more fun
together.' So I took his advice and soon afterwards we got
married.[102] Our wedding was very modest. The best man was
Sasha's friend Alexei Piterskikh; my bridesmaid was also one of
Sasha's friends. Sasha's father, Sergei Litkens, was present at the
ceremony as well.

Just before the wedding Sasha announced that we were going
on honeymoon to Lake Sevan in Armenia. I told my son about
our travel plans; but he did not say anything. It was the end of the
school year and his class was going to a summer camp in Moldavia,

102 This was in 1975.

and Sergei had decided to join his classmates. He had put a lot of effort into preparing for the camp: he had made a camping bag and trousers with his own hands. Just before leaving for the camp he came to me to say goodbye but suddenly let out a sob and whispered, 'I wanted so much to come with you and Sasha!' And rushed out of the door. I realised that I had just betrayed my son and burst into tears. I had forgotten that Sasha had originally promised to take Sergei to Armenia with us . . . I will never forgive myself for that betrayal . . . It was then, in the Moldavian camp, that Sergei got acquainted with his future wife Galina (who had gone there from another Moscow school) and became a man.

At first everything in our marriage went well: we often went to the theatre, to the cinema, or to the rehearsals at Sasha's theatre. One day my son, Sergei, went to the staff entrance of Sasha's theatre. The security lady asked him sternly, 'Who are you going to see?' Sergei proudly replied, 'I am going to see my father, his name is Sasha Litkens.' Later that lady told me smiling, 'I did not know you had such a big and polite son!' It was then that I realised how badly my son had been missing someone whom he could call Father.

Sasha was a very kind person and he really wanted to have a baby. I so much appreciated that and did my best, but, unfortunately, I failed: I had several miscarriages. I think it was as a result of what had happened during my first marriage. My son Sergei kept saying to me, 'Mummy, give me a little brother or a sister, I don't care who it will be!' He longed for a sibling so much but – in vain. I feel so sorry about that.

It was Sasha's second marriage, he had a son by his first wife who, for some reason, was reluctant to let Sasha see him very often.

I must say a little more about Sasha's father, Sergei Litkens. I knew him: he was a tall, sturdy man. After graduating from the KGB school he had gone to work for them. Unfortunately, shortly after World War Two, he took part in the arrest of a group of teenagers in the Voronezh District who were trying to fight Stalin's dictatorship.[103] Sergei Litkens was one of the investigators; the young people were arrested, tortured, and sentenced to long terms in prison or labour camps. Many years later, in the 1980s one of those teenagers, Anatoly Zhigulin, wrote a book about the case, called *The Black Stones,* in which he named all his torturers, including Sergei Litkens.[104] When we read the book we felt dreadful, especially my Sasha: he used to be so proud of his father. Sergei Litkens also read the book, which hit him very hard; he became very ill and died not long afterwards. This is yet another example of our cruel Russian history.

When we met Sasha was very poor: his salary as a stage director at the Moscow Youth Theatre was only ninety roubles per month, of which he had to pay thirty roubles in alimony to support his son. So he was left with a miserable sixty roubles which was totally insufficient to live a decent life. At that time my salary at Novosti and later at the Film Makers Union was one-hundred-and-seventy roubles per month. So we lived mainly on my earnings; besides which my parents always supported me. I also received alimony – ten roubles a month – from Slava. Out of my income I had to make regular payments for my flat in the 'co-operative' house in accordance with the terms of the installment agreement, and for the communal public utilities (electricity, water supply, etc.). Happily, at that time these services were relatively inexpensive.

103 In 1947 a group of high school students in Voronezh had set up an underground movement called the Young Communist Party dedicated to combating what they saw as the deification of Stalin and to returning the USSR to the original ideals of the Revolution. In 1948 twenty of them were arrested.
104 The book was published in 1989. After being tortured and imprisoned Zhigulin and the other students were sent to work in the forced labour camps of Kolyma. Zhigulin's book, *The Black Stones*, is widely regarded as one of the classic accounts of life in the Gulag Archipelago.

I did my best to get Sasha decent clothes: I bought him a very becoming trench coat, shoes, shirts, even socks and vests. On one occasion Sasha came home in the evening and gave me his salary or, rather, what was left of it: just three roubles. He explained that he had paid off his debts and then gone to the Actors Union restaurant with some of his friends, so at the end of the day all he had left was three roubles. The look on his face as he told me this was both kind and naïve . . . It was impossible to be angry with him. I laughed and said, 'All right, Sasha, we will live on your three roubles!'

I was grateful to Sasha for his tenderness, his kindness and lack of egotism, and for his great sense of humour. I was both his wife and his lover, I enjoyed cooking for him and taking care of him. He loved me very much, he loved my whole body and used to kiss me from head to toe. Sasha Litkens was the only man in my life who passionately wanted to have a baby by me, but miscarriages came one after the other. After two miscarriages Sasha, who so wanted a baby, sent me to the best gynaecologists and even to a specialised resort in Yalta in the Crimea but – in vain.

During my absence he fed my son and took care of my flat. But it was then that they started to drink liquor together in the evenings, after Sasha came home from his theatre: Sasha drank to relieve the stress of work and my son Sergei joined in to keep him company. They say that a Russian always needs to talk to someone, and alcohol loosens the tongue so well . . . When I came back from the Crimea I started to become really frightened for my son. As a result I eventually I asked Sasha to go and live with his mother. I told him, 'If you feel that you need me desperately come back.' Sasha replied in an arrogant manner, which was not typical of him at all, 'And if I never come back?' I said, 'Well, then so be it'. Sasha left and never came back.

I am sure we could have lived together until today but, unfortunately, Sasha was used to drinking and drank more and more often. He would come home at three or four in the morning after long get-togethers and drinking bouts with his friends. It was unbearable to watch a talented, intelligent, kind person killing himself. Finally we had to part because of his heavy drinking. Sasha, where are you? Please let me know! I wish I could hear from you . . . [105]

Bulgaria: First Time Abroad

It is not an exaggeration to say that for a Soviet citizen a trip abroad could be compared to a journey to the Moon. That's why when I was offered a chance to travel to Bulgaria and Romania I considered it a miracle. The trip was organised by the Novosti Press Agency and was scheduled for the beginning of January; our group was supposed to visit Bulgaria's capital, Sofia, then Varna, with its famous Golden Sands, and then return to Moscow via Romania.

Each Soviet person going abroad had to get permission from the local Communist Party and trade union authorities. It was a kind of test of dependability: a person was summoned to the local party committee, faced a panel of Party officials and had to answer their questions: about his/her life and work, about the country of destination, about current Soviet home and foreign policy. If the committee members were not satisfied with the answers they could refuse to give permission. After each 'candidate' was

105 Tamara and Alexander Litkens separated in 1978. In 1980 Litkens directed his one and only feature film and in 1982 became the director of a drama theatre in the city of Berezniki in the Perm Region, not far from the Ural mountains. In 1988 he was awarded the title Honoured Artist of Russia. Tamara lost touch with him completely and only recently found out that he died in 2004. After his death Litkens' former students wrote warmly of his unfailing kindness and talent.

approved, a tour group was formed. Each group was headed by a 'group monitor', a person appointed by a Communist Party organisation. The monitor had to be a Party member and was supposed to write a report after the trip was over. During the trip contact with foreigners was not approved of or even allowed.

When I entered the room to take my 'loyalty test' I was faced with a gathering of middle-aged and elderly party ladies headed by the chairman. All the ladies, for some reason, disliked me on sight and were clearly unwilling to give their consent. But then I somehow managed to win them over and got their approval.

It so happened that I fell ill, with a high temperature, right on the eve of our trip. But I hoped that I would be able to cope with my illness on the journey and quickly recover. However, on the train my fever got even worse, and I lay on the upper bunk weak and helpless.

Two nice young men from my group (later I called them 'my pages') noticed my desperate condition and took me under their wing. They took care of me throughout the trip.

In Sofia, as soon as we checked into the hotel, I pulled myself together and went out. In the street I was struck by the abundance of black eyes, black hair, black clothes, and swarthy faces.

I went into a small church. Surprisingly, the walls inside were dirty, nearly black with soot (perhaps from the church candles). I wondered how people could possibly pray and find consolation in such a sooty interior . . .

But my walk was more than my body could stand. I was still very ill and I spent the rest of the trip 'crawling' from one bus into another, and from one hotel into another. Now and then I braced myself and went out with the group.

Many Russian people celebrate New Year's Day twice: on the 31st of December and on the 13th of January, according to the old-style Julian calendar. So on 13th January our group decided to see the New Year in for the second time. I mustered my energy, got dressed in my best and went down to the hotel's dining-room. As I have said, I had always enjoyed dancing and was very good at it. At the party I danced a lot, attracting men's attention with my grace and agility. My two young 'pages' followed me everywhere. It was my triumph!

On the whole, I was glad to have been abroad, in spite of my illness and in spite of the annoyingly intrusive manner of our group monitor who watched us closely throughout and actually had the right to just barge into any of our rooms.

My work at the Novosti Press Agency involved numerous business trips. In May 1980, towards the end of my time at Novosti, I went with a team from the Agency to Baku, the Azerbaijani capital.[106] We were supposed to photograph several places in the city and then go to a highland lake called Lerik. When we reached Azerbaijan we were surprised to see orange and tangerine trees covered with fruit all around us: it looked so unusual and so beautiful!

In our group there was a cameraman, Tofik Shakhverdiev (his father was an Azerbaijani and his mother a Ukrainian) and an attendant whose name I don't remember. I do not exaggerate when I say that we were given a fantastic reception – as if we had been members of a royal family; people in the East receive valued guests in this way. We were given rooms in the magnificent Reception Home,[107] we were invited to a luxurious dinner with lots of fruit and delicious, wonderfully scented herbs; wine flowed like water. It was a pleasant surprise for me to see that Tofik Shakhverdiev did not drink anything but water.

After dinner we went for a walk. It was very dark, there were

---

106 Azerbaijan was incorporated into the Soviet Union in 1920 and only regained its independence in 1991.
107 A luxurious (by Soviet standards) official visitors' guest house.

no stars in the sky. All of a sudden our nameless attendant started molesting me. I screamed. And immediately I heard Tofik's voice: 'If you try that again I'll kill you!' and the sound of a thump on the head. I think it was in Tofik's blood: if a woman is not willing a man must not touch her, it's shameful! To this day I remember the noble protection of my cameraman, who inherited his code of honour from his father, who was killed in World War Two.

The Novosti Press Agency was often the venue of the first and only showings of many good films. In fact, almost all the most significant and creative Soviet films were shown only at either the Novosti Press Agency or at the Cinema House in Vassilievskaya Street.[108] I had the honour to work in both places, so I saw not only Western masterpieces but also the best of the Soviet movies. One has to bear in mind that almost all films of genius made during the Soviet period were put on the shelf for ten to twenty years, so viewers only got the chance to enjoy them many years after they had been made. This was what the USSR was like, such were the decisions made by the over-cautious bureaucrats of *GOSKINO* (The State Committee for Cinematography) and even by the top people in the country. That was the era we lived in and I hope that that time will never return for Russia.

I spent fourteen years at Novosti working with TV crews from the USA, France, Switzerland, and Great Britain. Then, in 1978, for some reason Novosti ran into trouble with the Soviet authorities who ordered that many of its staff were to be transferred to *TASS* (the Telegraph Agency of the Soviet Union). But my boss at that time, Margarita Vinogradova, who in fact hated me said, 'Only over my dead body will Samoilovich be transferred to

108 Cinema House in Moscow, the central club of the Film Makers' Union, which had several screening rooms. The general public were not permitted to purchase tickets for the screenings at Cinema House.

TASS!' (I still used my husband's name at that time). 'OK', I said and was instead transferred to work at the Film Makers Union.

I never regretted going there. As I've said, in the Cinema House they often showed the best and most interesting Soviet films, films which remained unknown to the general public for years. It was there that I first watched films by Andrei Tarkovsky, Andrei Smirnov, *Duck Hunt* (1979) with the brilliant Oleg Dahl starring, *Commissar*[109] (1967) with Nonna Mordyukova, Rolan Bykov and Raisa Nedashkovskaya which shocked and surprised the audience, *Twenty Six Days from the Life of Dostoyevsky* (1981) with the wonderful Solonitsyn as Dostoevsky, *At Home Among Strangers* (1974) by Nikita Mikhalkov and many others.

109 Based on one of Vassily Grossman's early short stories, the film depicts events during the Civil War which followed the Bolshevik Revolution. The film ran into trouble with the Soviet censors because it presented events in a manner which did not accord with the prescribed heroic picture of the Civil War. It was banned for twenty years and all but one of the screening prints of the film were destroyed. The director, Aleksandr Askoldov, was expelled from the Communist Party, banned from working in feature films for life and exiled from Moscow. Later, in 1988 during the period of perestroika, the film was reconstructed and shown at the Berlin Film Festival where it was awarded the Silver Bear Special Jury Prize.

Soviet Russia is the only country
That was killing itself.

ANDREI BITOV[110]

Trying to Understand

Soldered souls
And a cry in the night . . .
The past was left in the drink
That we could not swallow,
No matter how hard we tried.

We smelled the bloody anguish.
Then the bundle of roving darkness
Covered us all.

We pressed our palms to our temples
We prevented each other from pulling triggers.
Life touched us with its edge.
We lived in a basin riddled with holes
Believing that it was a ship.

We stayed aground in the basin
Gurgling for over seventy years
Turning tin into copper.

We were alchemists,
We used to turn the truth into lies.
We dragged the truth
And stabbed the knife
In between its shoulder-blades.

110 Andrei Bitov, born 1937, is an important contemporary Russian writer. By February 1988 Mikhail Gorbachev's reform of the Soviet Union was leading to the outbreak of civil wars and ethnic strife.

How can we cleanse ourselves
Of shy deafness?
What will protect us
Against the frightened dumbness?

How shall we open the truth
And stay alive?
What shall a wizard do
To make us wash with a clean tear?

14th February 1988

1978

More About My Son

When he was eighteen my son Sergei suddenly got married without saying anything to me.

I had gone on a business trip to Kronstadt[111] for two months. In Kronstadt I met some very nice and interesting people, all of them naval officers of the Baltic Fleet. I even attended a magnificent ball at the Officers' Club. Having always been a good dancer, I made the best of the dancing, especially as dance had always been more than just a dance for me. At the end of the ball a very young officer, just a boy, fell in love with me and even proposed to me. Thank God, I was clever enough to reject his proposal gently. His infatuation might have reminded me of my own early love for

---

111 Kronstadt: a town located on Kotlin Island, thirty kilometres west of St Petersburg in the Gulf of Finland. It is also St Petersburg's main seaport. Traditionally, the seat of the Russian admiralty and the base of the Russian Baltic Fleet which was located in Kronstadt to guard the approaches to St Petersburg. The historic centre of Kronstadt and its fortifications are part of a World Heritage Site.

Yevgeny Vassiliev. I tried to convince the young boy that he would meet his true love later and everything would be fine. To be honest, I was flattered by the attention of the young boy and said to myself, 'You still have got a lot of steam, old girl!'

The officers took me on a tour of all Kronstadt's forts. It was great fun! I told them that I had a son who loved St Petersburg very much and that I'd love him to see the forts, too. It was a deal!

Of course, I used to regularly phone my Mother from Kronstadt to ask how my parents and Sergei were doing. Then, at one point, Mother sounded very worried and said, 'Tamara, please come back soon: there is something wrong with Sergei'.

I returned to Moscow and immediately called Sergei and asked him to come to my work. We went out into the small garden and sat down on a bench. Suddenly I asked him, 'You are going to get married, aren't you?' Without a pause he replied, 'Oh, no, Ma, I won't get married before I turn twenty-seven'.

But my Zodiac sign is Pisces, and Pisces have a well-developed intuition. My question hit the target, but then I uttered a phrase I was to blame myself for later and even now still feel guilty about: 'Please bear in mind: I will not give my consent to your early marriage! You must first study for a profession, otherwise how are you going to provide for your wife and then for your children, as well?'

Later that day, back in our Moscow flat, my son came home with a huge bouquet of long-stemmed roses, my favourite. He stood in the kitchen doorway picking the floor with the toe of his shoe – he always behaved like that when he was feeling shy. I told him that he was expected in Kronstadt. Sergei beamed with joy and said that he, together with his friend Vasily, would leave for Leningrad the next day.

A few days later I received a telephone call from Kronstadt: one of the naval officers told me that Sergei had neither arrived in Kronstadt nor telephoned them. I thanked the officer and

Tamara's son, Sergei, in army uniform

Sergei at around the time of his marriage

immediately dialled the number of the Leningradskaya Hotel in Nevsky Prospekt. I asked if they had Sergei Samoilovich staying with them. The receptionist replied politely, 'Yes, and I am putting you through'. I heard Galina's sleepy voice on the other end. She recognised me, gasped, and gave the receiver to Sergei. Everything became clear. His companion was not his friend Vasily but his future wife Galina. I did not make a scene but simply mentioned the telephone call from Kronstadt: they were still expecting him. Sergei just said, 'OK, thank you, Ma'.

One night before Sergei was due to return from Leningrad I was sleeping and, all of a sudden, I felt as if something had made me sit bolt upright in my bed. With my eyes still closed, I fancied that I was reading a green crawling line, similar to the one that scrolled across the outside of the Izvestia building in Moscow carrying the latest news and information – what we called 'a green newspaper'.[112] With my mind's eye I clearly saw the following caption on the news line: 'Sergei is getting married'.

When I finally woke up, I went to the kitchen, put on the kettle and started knitting to calm myself down. I knew that so-called 'Japanese marriages' were popular in Moscow: some young people got married for only a couple of weeks or even days. Maybe that was the case with my son . . . ?

I went to my son's empty room. On the table I noticed a narrow sheet of paper with a list of different things to be taken somewhere. The first part of the list was written in Galina's handwriting and at the bottom of the page there were several items added by Sergei, including a suit. Now I understood everything. Later I learned that on that very night Sergei really had got married.

1980

At the Mental Hospital

So, Sasha Litkens had gone and soon after his marriage Sergei had been called up for his two years compulsory military service in the army. Suddenly I realised that I was alone . . . I continued working and usually came home late, about 9 or 10p.m. Opening the door of my flat I could hear only deafening silence which was intolerable. Not far from my place lived Sasha's friend, Leonid and his wife Faina. Once, finding I could stand the dull and deaf silence in my flat no longer, I ran round to their place. I pressed the button of the doorbell and when I saw Leonid opening the door for me I burst into tears. Leonid and his wife tried to find out

112 Izvestia: one of the two main Soviet national newspapers (the other was Pravda). Its editorial headquarters and printing presses were located in a tall building in Pushkin Square, close to the offices of Novosti.

what was wrong with me but I could not explain because I kept on sobbing. At last, after they had made me a cup of tea, I calmed down a little and was able to talk. Leonid said that Faina, who was a doctor, worked at a mental hospital where there was a rehabilitation unit which offered all kinds of treatments, medical manipulations and gymnastics. Faina diagnosed my condition as depression and asked, 'If I help you to get hospitalised will you agree to be treated?'

The mere mention of a mental hospital made my heart race with fear. But I realised that I really could not stay in my empty flat any longer, and nodded my agreement. The next morning Leonid picked me up and took me to the hospital. Faina had prepared all the necessary paperwork and I was led to a big two-storey brick building with a small garden, surrounded by a green fence. I filled in and signed all the necessary documents and found myself in a ward with twelve beds. The ceiling was very high: about five metres. I was shown my bed but was not allowed to lie down: they asked me first to sit down on a sofa in a hallway. I sat down and felt that I was falling asleep . . . That was how I became acquainted with Soviet psychiatry: at that time I knew nothing about the Soviet psychiatric system and only read about it much later.

All the doors in the building were permanently locked, only the doctors and nurses had keys with them. Every time a doctor or a nurse came in, they immediately locked the door behind them. We were allowed to walk in the garden. After each meal I was given a set of pills, all different sizes and colours; nobody explained to me what they were. Like all the other patients, I obediently swallowed them. After about a fortnight I found that the pills were making me aggressive: I would fly into rages over nothing and started to hate everyone. I would find an out of the way corner in some distant corridor and try to sleep, as far away as possible from the other patients. I was so frightened, terrified, by my own aggression that I decided I must see the doctor who was in charge of me at once and refuse to go on taking the pills. Faina worked in another department, the one for elderly people (I cannot imagine how much stamina and patience she must have needed in order to cope with such difficult work), so I could not get in touch with her immediately. However, I did manage to see her during one of my walks and my guess is that it was she who helped me to get to see my own doctor, as otherwise it was next to impossible. As I said earlier, all the doors were always locked and we had no access to the doctors.

A few weeks passed and then one day I was told that I was going to see one of the most famous Soviet psychiatrists (I don't remember his name). The professor turned out to be a lively, kind-hearted man. He talked to me for a while, asking me all kinds of questions and, finally, turned to address my doctor: 'I am sorry, colleague, but I can see no symptoms of depression here. This lady is just dead tired, exhausted, and what she badly needs is good sleep, not just at night but in the daytime as well. She has told you about this herself, hasn't she? She needs a lot of sleep! So please provide Tamara with this opportunity.' I was surprised that this simple truth was pronounced in my presence.

Yes, they did 'provide the opportunity'! The next day I was transferred to a small quiet ward with only three or four beds in it. A nurse made up an intravenous injection of a sleeping drug for me and said that I could get back to my multi-bed ward when I woke up. I immediately fell asleep. I woke up in the evening, had some dinner and returned to my original big ward. I was not given any more pills. After twelve days of living like that I felt my old self again, refreshed and free of all feelings of aggression.

In the meantime, my doctor asked me to call my former husband Sasha Litkens and invite him to come to the hospital for a talk. I called him and, strange as it may seem, he did come very soon. He had a long talk with my doctor, after which we parted very warmly. I thanked him for responding so quickly. Then the doctor called me and said, 'You know, your husband must be an excellent lover even if as a husband he is a failure.' I had to agree.

A month later I witnessed an event that terrified me. In the hall on the ground floor of our building there was a TV set which was always on in the evening. I had had hearing difficulties since I was a child, so I usually tried to sit as close as possible to the set. But, as a rule, all the best seats had already been taken. One evening, a middle-aged man kept a seat for me. I glanced at him gratefully. The same thing happened on the following few days.

One day his wife, a noisy, masterful woman, came to see him. After she left Victor (that was his name) came over to me and said shyly that before coming into the hospital he had worked as a goldsmith and that he would like to give me one of the things he had made. And he took out a pretty ring with a small stone.

One evening Victor was called out of the hall by a nurse. Some minutes passed and then, when I turned to look for him, I found that his seat was still empty. Another man told me that the nurse had asked Victor to go to his ward. 'OK,' I thought, 'maybe he was called for some medical treatment'. However, after a while I began to become concerned about him and plucked up the courage to go and look into his ward. There I saw Victor lying in his bed, staring dumbly in front of him. I waved my hand at him and slipped out quietly. Returning to the TV room, I suggested to my neighbour that Victor was just tired and wanted some rest. But my neighbour whispered into my ear, 'He has been given an aminazine injection!'[113] I was shocked. I already knew how this drug affected the human body, especially a person suffering depression, and that men are less resistant to its effects than women. The following day, when I saw Victor

---

113 Aminazine. A powerful drug used in the treatment of disturbed behaviour, to control psychotic illness and restless behaviour, especially in the elderly. It is sometimes used as a 'chemical cosh'.

again, he was nobody, he was a vegetable. One injection had been enough. The nurse whispered to me (as a big secret) that the injection had been given on the orders of Victor's doctor. I think that the doctors' policy was to prevent any close contact between the patients. Evidently, someone had reported on Victor. Later Victor used to habitually follow me during my walks and would sit beside me in the television room. But he remained speechless and emotionless.

Not long afterwards it was New Year's Eve. In the big canteen tables were set out in a long row, with benches on each side. Naturally, there were no alcoholic drinks, just juice, tea and sweets. I can't say that we had a lot of fun: everybody was looking into his or her plate. However, there was something that did attract everyone's attention, and that was my outfit! I had asked my mother to bring my charming white polka dot dress (the one I had worn for my wedding to Sasha Litkens) and my matching high-heeled open-toe sandals. I looked really pretty and I knew it!

Soon after that New Year's Day I returned home from the hospital. Another very complicated period of my life was over. But as we know, the end of one thing very often becomes the beginning of another . . .

2 June 1981

My Son . . . My Son

As I have said, my son Sergei married very young, soon after he had turned eighteen. His wife Galina was a bit older than he was, about a year and a half. She was the first woman Sergei had slept with – it happened when he was fourteen and they were both staying at the youth camp – and he had been under her influence ever since. Very soon after they were married Galina became pregnant and gave birth to their daughter, Anna.

It is interesting that my husband Sasha Litkens' first reaction to my son's wife, Galina, was not favourable. Like many stage directors he had a penetrating eye and was often remarkably good at reading a person's character. Shortly after Sergei got married to Galina I invited him and his wife to tea and I introduced Galina to Sasha. We had tea and talked about everything and nothing in particular. After the newlyweds had left Sasha was at the sink washing the dishes when he suddenly said, 'Gosh, where did our Sergei manage to find such a tart!?' By the way, my Father's first reaction to Galina was similar . . .

Their baby Anna was just seven months old when one day Sergei and Galina were invited to a friend's birthday party. I had gone away for two days to see some friends, so a young girl, an acquaintance of Sergei and Galina's, agreed to babysit Anna while they were at the party. I only found out what happened that evening much later.

I was told that at the party Galina got very drunk and started brawling. So my son took her home in a taxi, hoping that she would calm down, but she became even more violent.[114] She was screaming, 'I'm sick and tired of you, I am going to take the baby now and go to live with my mother!' I think my son must have been more than a little drunk as well. He said 'OK, you can go now, but without the baby and tomorrow, when you are sober, you can come back and take her if you still want to'. But

114 Alcoholism has been a major problem in Russia throughout its history despite repeated attempts by successive governments to curb it. In recent years alcoholism has been held responsible for a drop in the country's population, due to early deaths among people under fifty, especially young men. Tamara was not present during these events so her description of what happened is based on what she was told later. As a result her account may not be entirely accurate.

Galina just kept on screaming, lashing out and breaking things. It was a hot June night and the windows of the flat were open. Sergei kept imploring her to stop. Finally he said, 'If you don't stop this right now I am going to jump out of the window'. 'Jump out if you want to', was the reply. So he did. From the fifth floor. Galina went down into the yard, looked at him, then went back to the flat, took the child and left. The neighbours called an ambulance and the police. Sergei was taken to Moscow's Emergency Hospital No. 7.

Commentary

A neighbour, who also worked at Novosti and lived on the floor below, described what happened: 'My husband Felix and I were at home. It was a very hot night, all the windows were wide open. Suddenly I noticed something flying past our window. I thought one of the neighbours must have thrown something away and looked out. I froze – I saw a human body lying on the ground directly below our window. Terrified, I shouted, "Felix, come here a minute! It seems to be Sergei, Tamara's son." Felix also looked out and, shocked, yelled, "Call the emergency services and police. At once!" We immediately called the ambulance and the police. I couldn't take my eyes off Sergei's body spread-eagled on the ground. A little later I saw Galina, Sergei's wife, walk over to him and, without touching him, walk round his body, her hands held behind her back. Then she left. Disappeared. Later I watched as people in white coats approached Sergei and, lifting him with great care, put him into an ambulance.'

Another neighbour, Raisa, who is herself a doctor and who lives in the same block in the flat next to Tamara's, had been out to the theatre with her husband. Returning home late, they were surprised to find the staircase up to their flat packed with policemen and more policemen standing guard outside the door to Tamara's flat. With no idea what was going on, they entered their own flat and immediately telephoned Tamara. No one answered. Later neighbours told them what had happened – how Sergei had jumped out of the window and been taken away in an ambulance. 'We were unable to sleep all night. Yuri and I knew how much Tamara loved her son and how tenderly Sergei treated his mother. We also knew that Sergei had got married without telling his mother and how hard Tamara had taken the news. He had only been eighteen at the time and still had to do his military service and start on his career as an architectural technical draughtsman. We had two sons of our own and felt a deep sympathy for Tamara. And now this dreadful news! We didn't even know if Sergei had survived. Later we called the neighbour who had phoned the ambulance but she didn't know if Sergei was alive either.' It was only months later that Raisa saw Tamara and learned what had happened: how Sergei had been very seriously injured, that his spine and all the bones in both his arms and legs had been broken; how he had been rushed to Moscow's Hospital No. 7 and undergone a five hour long emergency operation.[115] For five days Sergei's life hung in the balance. On the sixth day

115 Tamara's description of what happened that evening is based on what she was told later by Sergei, Galina and various neighbours who heard or saw parts of what happened. Galina was probably too drunk to remember precisely what happened before the accident and afterwards was almost certainly in a state of severe shock. Sergei was also probably too drunk before he fell to be able to remember exactly what happened and after the fall he was too severely injured to be able to talk. Although it was a hot night and

Tamara received a call from the doctor in charge of Sergei to tell her that he would live. When the police visited the hospital to interview Sergei he accepted all the blame for the accident, probably so as to save Galina from any blame and make sure that their daughter Anna was not taken away from them.

the windows of Tamara's flat and other flats in the block were open, with the result that some of the neighbours heard some of what was happening in the flat and later saw Sergei spread-eagled on the ground, no one other than Sergei and Galina was present throughout or saw precisely what happened. As a result it is unlikely that anyone will ever know exactly what happened that night.

Tamara Continues the Story . . .

It is a miracle that Sergei survived. That he did so was due in the first place to the heroic and dedicated efforts of Dr Ivan Petrovich and the team of nurses in the Intensive Care Unit at Moscow's Hospital No. 7. I can never adequately express my thanks to them. Nor to my second husband Alexander Litkens who came with me when I went to visit Sergei in hospital for the first time, after he had been transferred from the Intensive Care Unit to a regular ward. As we entered the ward Alexander gently placed his hand over my mouth so that I would not scream when I first set eyes on my son, his impossibly thin body encased from head to foot in a kind of metal casing from the top of which his head emerged to reveal his guilty eyes looking anxiously towards me as we approached. It was a sight that will remain imprinted in my memory for the rest of my days.

I shall always remain grateful to my bosses at the Film Makers' Union, who cut through all the usual bureaucratic red-tape so as to arrange for me to have unlimited unpaid leave for as long as I needed in order to nurse my son. I shall also always owe a special debt of gratitude to Lyubov Kolokolova of the Ministry of Health. By good fortune I had met Mrs Kolokolova when I worked on a series of colour transparencies about the Health Service. I had found her a very kind, sympathetic person and we had got on well together. So when I approached her for help about getting the latest medicines for my son after his terrible fall she went out of her way to obtain a supply of reopolyglukin for Sergei, a medicine and special nutrient essential for speeding his recovery from such serious injuries. She provided boxes containing dozens of bottles of it for Sergei, plus special plaster of Paris gypsum bandages for setting his broken bones. It was absolutely impossible to buy any of these things in normal pharmacies during that era of total Soviet shortages. Later, after Sergei was transferred to Kurgan, she continued to arrange for the medical supplies he needed to be sent out there.

I shall also remain eternally grateful to Sergei's grandfather, General Samoilovich, for the way he immediately got involved in the tragedy and did everything possible to help my son. It was he who got permission for me to sleep in the hospital so that I could remain near Sergei while he slept. Later General Samoilovich was instrumental in negotiating Sergei's transfer to Dr. Ilizarov's world-famous, pioneering orthopaedic and trauma centre in Kurgan and made arrangements to have Sergei transported there.[116] He helped me again a year later when the time came to arrange for Sergei to be taken back to Moscow.

In Kurgan Sergei was treated by the great trauma expert and

116 Kurgan is about one-thousand-two-hundred miles southeast of Moscow in southern Siberia.

orthopaedic surgeon Dr. Gavriil Ilizarov himself. The fact that Sergei was enabled to walk again was due to the skill of Dr Ilizarov and his brilliant team of nurses and physiotherapists.[117] Sergei and I also owe a huge debt of gratitude to all my and Sergei's friends who came daily to see him in Hospital No. 7 in Moscow and later, when we left Moscow for Kurgan, wrote both of us letters and even sent us money. In Hospital No. 7 in Moscow the kitchen staff were wonderful and readily agreed to allow me to use their kitchen to cook special meals for my son. Once my son had recovered enough not to have to be fed through a drip my Father brought food to the hospital every day so that he could have the sort of food he normally had at home.

Later, when Sergei and I went to Kurgan for treatment in Dr Ilizarov's clinic, my Mother regularly cooked specially nutritious meat preserves which she packed into three-litre glass preserving jars. In the city of Kurgan we would not have survived without my parents' help. Every two weeks they would send us money and food via the train conductors (in 1981 it was absolutely impossible to buy any of the right kind of food in Kurgan's food stores). My Mother would entrust her jars of specially prepared meat preserves to the conductors on the Trans-Siberian railway who conveyed them safely, at little or no cost, from Moscow to the station in Kurgan where I collected them. My second husband Sasha Litkens' sister Lyudmila also prepared meat preserves to her own special recipe which she also packed into three-litre preserving jars and sent to Kurgan. We will never be able to thank all these people enough for everything that they did for us.

117 Gavriil Ilizarov (1921–1992): pioneering orthopaedic surgeon, who invented equipment for use in surgical procedures to lengthen or reshape limb bones, treat complex and open-bone fractures and treat fractures that had become infected and failed to join after treatment using other, conventional, techniques.

Tamara and Sergei outside Dr Ilizarov's clinic

When Sergei's spine and legs were more or less recovered he enrolled in the Department of Restoration at the Moscow Higher Art School. After graduating from it he started working for the Moscow Patriarchate, renovating churches. It was not an easy job. He had to work high up on scaffolding – otherwise it was impossible to gild the domes of the churches. It is a craft that requires great patience, concentration and a love of the work.

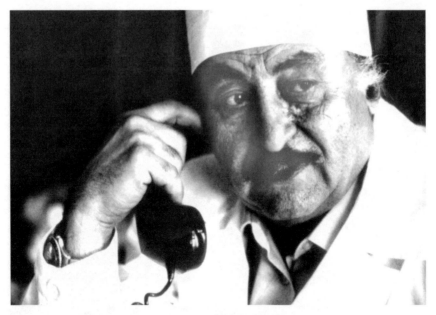

Dr Gavriil Ilizarov

Vladimir Vysotsky once said in one of his songs, 'The domes in Russia are covered with genuine gold, so that God pays more attention to us'. Yes, Russia deserves God's attention. Let God give this country His blessings and . . . luck. I am praying for it.

I think highly of my son because of his kindness, sense of humour, and staunchness, although I know, being disabled, his life is not easy. But I don't think that anyone who meets him or works with him ever guesses that he is disabled. Sergei never complains. I am proud of him.[118]

118 Tamara's friend Luba Ioffe says that even today, more than thirty years later, if anyone mentions Sergei's accident, Tamara becomes very nervous and 'seems to live through it again and again . . . ' Later Sergei and Galina had two more children, Helen and Petya. Sadly Petya died in 1991, aged just thirteen months.

Our Vysotsky in Siberia

It was while I was in Kurgan in 1981 that I really heard the songs of Vladimir Vysotsky for the first time, a year after his death.[119] One of the patients of Dr Ilizarov's clinic, Anatoly Vyatkin, had a large collection of audio tapes of songs by Vysotsky. Until then I had known Vysotsky simply as a stage and film actor who also composed and performed his own songs.

It was Anatoly's idea to organise a concert of Vysotsky's songs in the hall of the city library. All the young patients from Dr Ilizarov's clinic were invited. I helped Anatoly as much as I could. In particular, I contacted the director of a local factory and persuaded him to lend us a large bus in which to take the patients from the clinic to the concert. The bus was packed: some people had two crutches, some had one, others just clung to the rails so as not to fall down . . . There was enough room in the hall for everybody. Anatoly brought a large tape recorder and the audience sat still listening to their favourite songs.

I must mention that I had heard Vysotsky before this, but the recordings had been of such poor quality that I had not been able to understand half of the words. But there, in Kurgan, every word

119 Vladimir Vysotsky (1938–1980). Vysotsky has been called the Russian Bob Dylan. Like Dylan, he expressed the feelings of the young and disenchanted youth of the 1960s. But unlike Dylan, because he was working in the Soviet Union and frequently gave voice to ideas that were not approved of by the Soviet authorities, many of his recordings had to be released clandestinely. Nevertheless he had a huge fan base and exerted enormous influence which lasts to this day. He was also an accomplished actor who appeared in numerous films and stage productions, notably at Lyubimov's Taganka Theatre. His early death was due to many years of alcohol abuse.

he sang was intelligible, and my son and I were sitting upright, with our fists clenched tight: I cannot imagine how else one can listen to Vysotsky's immortal words, words that reach to the bottom of one's heart! Sergei, who had been brought to the concert in a car, was happy: he held his breath and was all ears. And I was happy too, because we had succeeded in giving so many young people (mostly boys) the chance to enjoy the wonderful songs. The people of Kurgan were very special: kind and responsive. Money was not the top priority for them: nobody charged us anything for renting the library hall! It is not for no reason that Kurgan is a part of *my* Siberia!

Later, after my parents had sent me another parcel – this time with our autumn clothes – I dressed my son, again asked the director of the factory for the use of a car and a driver and took Sergei out into the country. I am so grateful to the factory director who made it possible for us to have the car for that day!

It was a beautiful autumn day. The driver drove us to a pond with a large lawn in front of it, surrounded by a magnificent forest. By that time Sergei was using only one crutch and a walking stick. We were being silly and laughed a lot. My son was completely happy and very handsome. That day I again felt at home in *my* Siberia!

When I first learnt about Vysotsky's death, on 25th July 1980, the first thing I did was to write a long letter to the Government Committee for State Prizes. I wrote, 'Vladimir Vysotsky had a deep understanding of the Russian soul. His songs about the most terrible war of the twentieth century are strikingly true. His lyrics are full of humanity, spiritual strength, and overwhelming love for his Motherland. I cannot imagine anyone who deserves a State Prize as much as he does'.

However, I realised that our people, from Moscow to the Far East, had already awarded Vysotsky the highest possible prize: the

Vladimir Vysotsky

nation's love. His unique husky voice could be heard in every flat, from every window and even from the portable tape recorders of passers-by.

Naturally, I did not get a reply to my letter. But, nevertheless, several years later Vysotsky was posthumously awarded the State Prize of the USSR.[120]

---

120 The State Prize of the USSR was awarded to leading figures in the arts, sciences, literature and architecture for work that was deemed to have advanced the Soviet Union or the socialist cause. The first ever officially published volume of Vysotsky's poems did not appear until a year after his death. It instantly sold out and had to be re-printed many times. Over the years since then many more volumes of his work have appeared. Today there is a much visited Vysotsky monument and museum in central Moscow. Each year, on his birthday, Vysotsky festivals are held throughout Russia.

Tamara checking transparencies at   *Tamara in 1987*
the Film Makers' Union

My Friend Andrei Soloviev

One day in the late 1980s, after I had left Novosti and was working
in the editorial office for colour transparencies at the Film Makers'
Union, a handsome young man came into the office and said he
wanted to work for us. He had his own camera and was willing to
take photographs. His name was Andrei Soloviev.[121]

At that very moment I was looking for someone to photograph
the Donskoy Monastery: we were preparing a series of trans-

121 Andrei Soloviev: Experienced Russian war photographer who covered
    many conflicts during the break up of the Soviet Union, including
    wars in Nagorno-Karabakh, Tajikistan and South Ossetia. He also
    covered the collapse of the Ceauşescu regime in Romania and the first
    Iraq war. He was killed by sniperfire during the war in Abkhazia in
    1993. He won many awards, including the World Press Photo Prize.

parencies devoted to the monastery.[122] I supplied him with plenty of photographic film although we only needed to publish twenty-four pictures.

The Donskoy Monastery is a remarkable place. It has long been used as the burial site for famous people. So there are the graves of many of the great Russian writers, poets and painters. The monastery also contains the graves of relatives of Pushkin, Turgenev's mother, Leo Tolstoy's grandmother and many others. Some of the tombstones were designed by famous architects and sculptors. The monastery was not active in Soviet times but its territory, premises and the old cemetery were still regarded as worth seeing and admiring.

A few days later Andrei brought us two completed rolls of film in which every shot was a work of art! For colour photography and, specifically, for colour transparencies, the correct choice of light and shadow is very important. Besides, the result can be different depending on the time of day when the shots are taken. From his very first assignment with us, it was clear that Andrei was not just a skilful photographer but also a subtle artist. Naturally, I gave him one task after another and thought of myself as the person who had discovered his talent.

But one day Andrei came into the office and, looking down so as not to meet my eyes, said, 'Tamara, I've got another job: I am going to work for TASS.'[123]

---

122 The Donskoy Monastery in Moscow was founded in 1591 to commemorate Moscow's deliverance from the advance of the army of Khan Kazy-Girey from the Crimea. Originally it was a fortress intended to protect Moscow from invaders from the south. The cathedral was completed, on the orders of Boris Gudunov, in 1593 to house the icon of Our Lady of the Don.

123 TASS: the Telegraph Agency of the Soviet Union, the central news agency of the Soviet Union which had a monopoly on official state information.

Andrei Soloviev

I gasped. I knew that working for TASS would not involve any artistry. There he would be confined to taking mainly black and white news agency photographs.

This was at the beginning of the stormy, even crazy, era in our history: perestroika, crowds of people on Moscow's streets, Boris Yeltsin, the attempt to storm the Moscow TV centre, crowds in Baku, Vilnius, Tbilisi . . . One of the most tragic events was the war in Abkhazia, which broke out suddenly and seemed incomprehensible to us.[124]

This was also a period of turmoil in Andrei's private life. He had two nice boys whom he loved dearly, but, for reasons unknown to me, there was something wrong in his relationship with his wife . . . In order to ease his mental pain, he did his best to go to especially dangerous places. In fact, before his death he had been

124 1992–3. War waged between Abkhazian separatists and Georgian government forces trying to prevent the creation of an independent break-away state.

to all the former Soviet Union's trouble spots, taking with him both his camera and a submachine gun.

I saw all the political photos that he took for TASS. Yes, they were black and white but, at the same time, so expressive that it made one shudder all over. Some of the pictures were in colour but they also portrayed wars or armed conflicts. That was what the crazy 1990s were like, and that was how they transformed artistry into severity.

At one point Andrei was wounded: his arm was injured. After receiving some treatment, he rushed back into the thick of things – this time to Abkhazia where a war was under way. When we – everybody who knew and loved him – learnt about his death it was like a thunderbolt. Andrei was killed by a shot to the head. It happened in September 1993. Andrei was just forty years old. Nobody discovered who had shot him or who had ordered the shooting. The main thing was that a handsome man and a nice chap, the father of two boys, had died.

The civil funeral service took place in the TASS assembly hall. I went to it. A lot of women were crying. So was I. Then somebody pushed me forward to Andrei's coffin and asked me to say a few words. I wiped away my tears and talked about his early work: how wonderful and promising it was, how much taste there was in each of his photos. 'There will be other talented photographers, but people are unique and there will be no one to equal Andrei in either his inspiring work or his unmatched kindness'. With these words I broke into tears again and stepped aside, hiding behind the many people who had come to say goodbye to Andrei.

Andrei Soloviev was buried in the Vagankovo Cemetery, in its central aisle, to the left of the church.[125] When you visit the

125 The burial place of many famous Russian artists and poets including the singer and musician Vladimir Vysotsky and the famous poet Sergei Yesinin, the husband of the dancer Isadora Duncan.

cemetery do not miss his grave: bow your head before the man with a camera who defended freedom, democracy and his two boys.

How I Attempted a Suicide

It was 1990. My Mother used to come to my place from time to time – to see me and help me about the house. Sometimes she would stay with me overnight. One day I came home from work and found my Mother sitting on the sofa looking unwell. I knew she had heart problems and I always kept some heart medicine in my first-aid kit.

I asked Mother, 'What's wrong? Is it your heart?' But she remained silent. I offered her the heart drops but she shoved away my hand in which I was holding the glass with the medicine, which fell and smashed. In old age my Mother had become rather fretful, so I was not surprised. What did surprise me was that she refused to talk to me. I kept asking her, 'Is it the wrong medicine? Shall I get another one from the pharmacy?' She did not reply, but it was evident that there was something wrong with her. I ran to the pharmacy to get another medication, came back and tried to give it to her, but the scene with the glass was repeated: Mother did not want to take it from me.

In desperation I phoned my son Sergei and asked him to come immediately. 'Your grandma is freaking out, I don't know what to think, please come now!' I said.

Sergei soon arrived. He entered the room where my Mother was sitting and closed the door behind him, leaving me in the kitchen. They talked for a while, then he came out of the room, came over to me and said, 'Mother, you are unkind, do you know that? And I am very tired, I am going home now.' With these words he left.

I did not understand what he meant and was just shocked by Sergei's words. It was like a death sentence. I could hardly breathe. I thought, 'If he really thinks that, I have nothing to live for.' The decision came the minute Sergei left. I had some tranquillisers in my home medicine chest, so I took forty pills of Seduxen[126] and thirty Pipolphen pills.[127] After that I had enough time to write a letter addressed to all the members of my family, including my grandchildren, in which I sent them my best wishes. Then I fell asleep. It seemed to me that I had slept for days, although in fact it was several hours. At one point I woke up, called my friend Lilia, told her what had happened and then fell asleep again. When I woke up for the second time I saw Lilia, her husband and my neighbour Raisa (who had a key to my flat) beside my bed.

My friend Lilia took me to hospital. The doctor said, 'You must thank your head. Because of your habitual migraines your body was accustomed to different pain relievers. That is why the amount of tablets you took was not enough to kill you and you woke up.' A few days later Sergei came to see me. We were sitting silently next to each other in the hospital hall for about forty minutes. At last I said, 'You seem to have nothing to say. Neither do I. Come again when you find some words for me.' The next day he came again, this time with flowers, and asked me to forgive him. I did.

---

126 A tranquilliser similar to Valium.
127 An anti-histamine used to treat allergies and prevent vomiting, especially motion sickness.

Whose Fault Was It?

And everywhere fateful passion invades,
And from one's fate there's no escape.

Pushkin, *The Gypsies*

Mother planted a shoot.
The shoot struck root.
The crown gained strength.
Now Mother is sitting beside it
And the tree has grown to be Mother's equal . . .

The young tree rustles elegantly.
It keeps on growing.
Sometimes the wind rocks it
Making it stagger as if from wine.

Then the crown grows wild,
The branches crack,
The leaves fall down,
Fall down to the ground.

Mother watches sadly
His early grey hair.
She is afraid he will bring disaster upon himself.

Sometimes she scolds him mercilessly
For the sins of his young days.
But those sins are inevitable for those
Who grow too big for their routine path.

One day Mother wakes as if from a rude shove.
Somebody is knocking at her heart.

In the distance the crown of her gallant son
Is rustling . . .

But instead of bright green
She sees his grey hair against the blue sky:
'Mother, why have you sometimes been unkind to me?'

'Can it be my fault?'
She thought with anguish and terror . . .

Switzerland at Last

In 1995 I received an invitation from Jean-Luc to visit Switzerland. He also asked me to get a French visa because he was going to show me Paris as well. That was something! On top of which, he told me that he had already paid for my return air tickets to Geneva and that all I had to do was to pick them up at the airport ticket office (he even gave me the number of the desk and the name of the girl who had my tickets). I was amazed at such a luxurious gift!

Very soon I found myself at Geneva airport. Jean-Luc met me and quickly brought me to his home where I met his wife Mariam and their three children: a girl and two boys. The dinner was gorgeous. The table was covered with a snow-white table cloth and beautifully laid. I was particularly struck by the water in the jug: it was as clear as a tear and very tasty. When they told me that the water was from the tap I was astonished: in Moscow tap water can smell of anything, mainly of chlorine, lots of which is used in the reservoirs from which the flats in Moscow get their water.

Jean-Luc wanted to show me as much as possible in the ten days I was due to stay with him. The next day we went to the celebrations of the Swiss National Day, marking over seven-hundred years of Swiss independence. My first full day in Geneva had a dramatic ending. The celebrations took place near Lake Geneva where we spent nearly the whole day under the hot summer sun. I had quite forgotten to ask for a hat and was wearing just a ribbon round my head. The festival was a great success but when I came back home I suddenly collapsed on to the sofa groaning with a terrible headache. I was just praying to God that I would not vomit — as was usually the case with my migraines. I inherited this horrid condition from my Father who had suffered migraines until the end of his days.

I heard Mariam enter the room where I was lying on the sofa and carefully remove several books which I had put under my head instead of a pillow. She quietly replaced the books with a real pillow. I groaned because even the lightest touch to my body gave me pain. That is what this strange disease, known since the time of Hippocrates, is like.

The migraine prevented me from seeing Paris where Jean-Luc was planning to take me the next day. When I got up and came downstairs for lunch it became clear that I was not going to see Paris even though it was so close! I somehow reconciled myself to the fact even though I had a French transit visa in my passport.

Migraine

One cannot describe it,
It is beyond comprehension,
Your mouth is locked
Only your eyes are exhaling tears.

Yours arms hang loose beside your body.
Your eyes are reflecting window panes.
Your soul is exhausted with loneliness
And you are a toy of fate in fetters.

Day whirls after day.
As though in a torture chamber,
They are twisting your empty body
For the pleasure of the evil genius beyond us.

At last: slowly, slowly
The boiling lava calms down
Again the springs are spouting at your temples,
Making sakura wreaths
On the threshold of a possible life.

I asked Jean-Luc to show me the house in Geneva where Henri lived. Jean-Luc drove me there in his car. I went up to the front door, looked down the list of the names of the residents and found 'Henri Brandt'. Each name had a doorbell button next to it. I stroked the button several times but never dared to press it and then returned to the car. When Jean-Luc asked me 'Why?' I replied, 'Because he is married.' The next night I had a dream: I do press the button, fly up the stairs, Henri throws open the door and embraces me, we sit down and talk, talk endlessly and excitedly, telling each other about the years we have lived without each other.

In order to 'compensate' for Paris, Jean-Luc took his family and me to the Alps in his car; to the beautiful Alps that we, in Russia, had only seen in films or on postcards. The air in the Alps was transparent and fragrant. The roads were wonderful, and our car seemed to fly. My feelings were unforgettable: high speed, magic landscapes and dear friends beside me!

On the way, we stopped at Jean-Luc's *dacha. Dacha* is a Russian word; Jean-Luc called it 'our old house'. It was quiet, warm and sunny. The little house looked like an old Russian house and – like everything else in Switzerland – looked very modest from the outside and was very convenient inside where everything was done to make human life easy and comfortable. Yes, it was really beautiful!

Then we rode in a cable car in the mountains. Oh, what a sight it was: mountains below us, mountains above us, all wearing snow 'hats'. Looking around I kept thinking, 'Lord, why have you sent me such a wonderful gift? Do I really deserve it?' Sometimes I was afraid even to breathe – my delight was so great!

In the Alps we ate ice-cream sitting on wooden benches round a wooden table, looking admiringly at the beauty everywhere around us. Then we went to an open-air museum: an old town with a cobblestone street lined on both sides with tiny workshops where craftsmen were making all sorts of lovely little things. Jean-Luc's youngest son went over to one of the craftsmen and asked him about something. A few minutes later he proudly gave me a small penknife with my name – 'Tamara' – engraved on it. How happy I was! It is so wonderful to be loved and cared for! My dear, dear Jean-Luc, my dear 'Baron'! I will always remember that fantastic trip to the mountains when we wandered about the town, sat down at tables on the river bank and indulged in ice-cream more than once. Looking at me Jean-Luc kept saying, 'You are exactly like your granddaughter Anna: she was just mad about ice-cream!'

I was eating my ice-cream and looking at the garlands of flowers hanging down from the windows. It seemed to me that that was the way paradise ought to look! I will always be grateful to Jean-Luc and his family for the heavenly days that to me seemed endless. My goodness, how desperately I wanted not to have to leave! My Russia is a beautiful country but Switzerland was and will forever be my dream!

To my Swiss Friend Jean-Luc Nicollier

I have a friend in far-off Europe,
Jean-Luc by name.
He is tall, stately, and handsome.

By the way, he is a baronet.
The baronet is married to Mariam from Persia.
They have three children
And, I guess, grandchildren will be smiling at them soon.

It was my native Siberia that made us friends.
The country that he had never seen before
And that conquered his heart once and forever.

I vividly remember everything
That we experienced in the thick *taiga*
Among beautiful pine-trees
And people who differ so greatly from all others
In their kindness and smiling souls . . .

I also remember the wonderful Geneva,
Surrounded with beautiful nature . . .
All those European beauties
Were presented to me generously
By Jean-Luc, a friend of mine.

I will always be grateful to him and his family
For inviting me to the Country of Wonders,
Of the Alpine Mountains,
Of Crystal Waters,
Of Fresh Breath . . .

Not long ago our television showed a documentary about the famous Russian actress Zoya Fyodorova who, in 1945, had an affair with an American and, because of that, was imprisoned 'for espionage' for eight years. I cried watching the film as I saw so much in common with my own story.

Henri was absolutely sure that we would stay together and made me believe in our future, too. My first doubts arose when the USSR sent tanks into Prague: I supposed that our government would hardly allow us to be together. But later, when Henri came to Moscow and during our trip to Sochi, I regained confidence. Whoever we met in Sochi, Henri always introduced me as his wife. Back in 1969 I was unaware of Zoya Fydorova's story. Probably, if we had known it we would have been more cautious . . . Of course, the outcome of our love affair was much less harsh: I was not sent to prison, my dream was just destroyed and buried. Our lives (mine and Henri's) were ruined. Henri passed away long ago. But I still miss him, even today, and I am sorry I did not have a baby by him. As long as I am alive the memory of Henri will live, too. Time was trying to kill our love but was unable to. Love turned into a beautiful legend and legends do not die, they live longer than their characters!

Jean-Luc told me that there were no photographs of me to be found in Henri's flat after his death. While I knew that Henri had taken a lot of pictures of me. Maybe he had destroyed the pictures because he did not want anybody else to meet his only and true love . . . That's only my assumption.

25 September 2004

(my Mother's birthday)

You are up in the clouds
Like a Japanese butterfly . . .
You hope the sakura will not shed its blossom
And may someday give you shelter
On that same twig.

Life, stay here a while,
Please!
I am both serious and smiling
You see that I haven't finished all my work.

Things to do surround me,
They crowd closer and closer.
My health gets weaker every day,
On the way to nowhere.

My parents have gone
And are silent up in the sky.
My friends are leaving like
Circles on the water,
They nod to me from there.

Today I understand a lot.
I do understand a lot today.

That is why I ask you,
'Life, stay here for a while,
Please! I beg you!'

I promise to use the rest of the days properly,
Giving my whole self to those I love.

To Whom the Bell Tolls

How much silence there is around!
We are almost forgiven
For the fever
Of the terrible Chernobyl days.[128]

We forgive ourselves for everything,
We forgive others nothing!
External events –
They strike others, not me.

Then for whom do the bells toll
And sometimes sing their grey-haired song?

Trains cry on their way
With their unseen, unadopted tears . . .

Our bell tolls only in our minds,
Its sound is lost in the blue sky.

No one can drag the souls
Out of their lethargy.

Having worked at the Novosti Agency for many years and later at the Film Makers' Union of the USSR, I had acquired fairly good journalistic skills and some of the pieces that I had written had been published abroad. But I discovered my need to write creatively all of a sudden, following the terrible stress I that I had experienced with my son.

128 The worst nuclear accident in history occurred on 26th April 1986 when one of the reactors at a power station in Chernobyl, in the Soviet Republic of Ukraine, exploded.

After his recovery I had started to get ill more and more often and more and more seriously, even though I had endured all the earlier hardships with courage and determination, and with the humour which my son had appreciated so much. To put it briefly, once the danger was over, I had begun to fall to pieces. It was then that I suddenly discovered my need to express myself creatively. First came prose, and then, suddenly, there was poetry. Where on earth did they come from? I don't know. A line from a poem would come at night, in a dream, and like a quiet guest, would wait for me to write it down. I would grab a piece of paper and a pencil and write frantically. Sometimes an entire poem would come into my head, and I hurried to write it down, afraid I would lose it. I do not know who was directing my hand. I sometimes think it was the Lord, and I was just obeying His will like a good child. Then, quite unexpectedly, I became totally disabled, and now it was my son's turn to buy me a walking stick with four 'paws' that became my friend. And I acquired wonderful new friends (not many, but they support me staunchly) who decided to publish a book of my poetry without any thought of the cost. Of course, one has to pay for everything, such is the age we live in. We cannot choose the time for living . . .

So, with their encouragement, I decided to take the risk and have it published.[129]

---

129 In 2006 Tamara's friend Svetlana Kharlampidi paid twenty-thousand roubles (about four hundred pounds) to a printer to have five hundred copies of the book printed and Tamara reimbursed her over a period of years.

To the Light Girl Called Svetlana

A tiny kitten is drowning in the sea.
A girl in a boat sees it.
She rows with all her might
Battling through the waves.

She wants to save the kitten,
To give him a chance to survive.
The kitten clutches her.
Now it is safe.

The girl presses the kitten to her chest,
She is walking along the shore,
All wet with salty water
And smiling to the kitten and to herself.

She hides her face in the wet but warm fluffy nubble
And is telling him something gently.
While the happy grey kitten is purring its song once again.

The girl did not tell anybody
About her feat.

To Conclude

I could have lived – while I was still young in years – in Romania or in Bulgaria or in Norway, or even in Switzerland, right in the centre of Europe. My God, why am I, nevertheless, living in Russia? Maybe because I was always proud of my large country... Now that pride has vanished into smoke, I only quietly rejoice in remembering my birthplace – Siberia.

Old Age

'Getting old is sad,
But it is the only way
To live a little more . . . '

Nicolai Amosov[130]

Old age is a slow parting,
A melancholy waltz of expectation,
A transient turn of recognizing myself in many others
And others in myself.

One who lived without Communion
Who used to cry silently longing for cleansing
Who wanted to feel the heartbeat of others inside oneself.

Old Age is a rise and fall,
A listless retardation,
A spellbound whirling of a maple leaf
From skies to the ground.

130 Nicolai Amosov (1913–2002). Famous doctor and author of the book, *Thoughts On Health*, a best-seller in the USSR.

Old Age is the inevitable,
Devastatingly irresistible,
Something viscous and feeble and durable
Similar to a tin soldier in his readiness.

Blessed are those who will be able
To get over this long moment
And become the murmur of a birchwood
In spring . . .

Our old people are going away.
They are leaving quietly, silently,
Without arguing either with the time
Or with the children who, though, may be far from them . . .

In my youth we had our own old people.
We used to shout while they were quiet,
We used to grumble: any word pronounced by the elderly
Caused a storm of protest.

We thought ourselves cleverer, smarter, faster
Than our old people.
We certainly did not think of the transient moment
That would make everybody equal.

Then the day of reckoning comes:
Repentance, tears, desperation,
Reluctance to live,
Friends would turn their backs on you:
They do not want you the way you are today . . .

A person can be judged by the way
The old people around him are leaving.
If their departure is like time-lapse filming,
The fine thread will stretch and not tear . . .

Then everything turns into *farce majeur.*
Old age is a litmus test of your pride in truth.

Desire

I'd like to leave in this way:
To vanish into thin air
Without tears and sobs,
Without funeral processions,
Without half-withered flowers,
Without dead wreaths.

Then the transparent palm of the water
Would join the sun, the stars, the moon,
And the sad, white glance of my son.
My earthly joy.

Tamara's Life Today
by her friend, Luba Ioffe

I am afraid that readers who do not know today's Russia well cannot imagine what it means to be a lonely old-age pensioner with numerous health problems living there. I say 'lonely' because, in spite of the fact that Tamara's son and his family also live in Moscow, they see each other very seldom. As I see it, there is a striking contradiction between what she writes about her son and the life he allows, or is compelled because of his work, to let her live. A person like Tamara is helpless and totally dependent on the good will of those who stay in contact with her.

Tamara lives in a one-bedroom flat in a distant part of Moscow. Her flat is full of old stuff – old furniture, old photos, old tableware . . . 'Old' does not mean 'valuable' here; 'old' means that the things have lived too long and are worn out. The flat badly needs renovation, but this is out of the question.

Tamara's eyesight has deteriorated drastically over the past few

On facing page: Tamara today, and above: Galina and Sergei today

years. She can only read with the help of a magnifying glass. Writing this book was like playing a blindfold game of chess for her: although she used black felt pens, she was unable to re-read what she had already written. Tamara cannot watch TV but she can listen to it.

Several years ago Tamara broke her leg and the fracture did not knit properly, that's why it takes her a lot of effort to move around. She seldom goes out and then mainly in summer. She cannot walk further than the garden of her block of flats. It is always a problem for Tamara to go to the doctor: she needs someone to take her there in a car. This 'someone' is her son, but he may be too busy or may be away on a business trip in another city, so Tamara has to wait for weeks, even months, for a chance to see the doctor. Such was the case about two years ago when several months passed before she could see a dentist. If something urgent happens she calls an ambulance.

A social worker comes in twice a week and brings her food, medicines and other things. Tamara gives her money to buy things for her. Several times a week a nurse comes in to take care of some

Tamara and her granddaughter Alyona

of Tamara's current medical problems – to give her injections and so on. Both the social worker and the nurse are provided by the state, Tamara does not have to pay for their services.

Tamara's pension is about fifteen-thousand roubles (three hundred pounds) a month, which is considered not bad for an old-age pension in Russia but is, in fact, very little. Being a pensioner and a disabled person, she is entitled to discounts when she pays for communal public services or for medicines. As a pensioner she also has the right to use public transport free, but she cannot make use of this right because she is physically unable to get to the bus or on and off the underground.

The telephone is the thing that connects her to the outer world. She appreciates people calling her and likes talking to them.

I may be wrong, but it seems to me that Tamara lives in the past and by the past. That is why working on this book has been like a ray of light in her routine struggle for survival; it makes her life meaningful and gives her a chance to re-live certain episodes and, maybe, to understand them better.

Photograph Credits

(All photos copyright of Tamara Astafieva [T. A.] unless otherwise stated. They come from her family albums or, where marked, M.D., from Michael Darlow's private collection of photographs of his time working with Tamara in Russia. Unless otherwise stated, the identity of the individual photographers of these photos is not known. All other rights holders or sources identified after each photo.

Front Cover Photo – T.A.

Page 30 (*Top left*) Tamara's father and mother – T.A.

Page 30 (*Top right*) Tamara's uncle Tima – T.A.

Page 30 (*Bottom left*) Tamara's Aunt Anna – T.A.

Page 30 (*Bottom right*) Tamara's parents *c.*1944 – T.A.

Page 31 (*Top left*) Tamara's mother – T.A.

Page 31 (*Top right*) Tamara's father

Page 31 (*Bottom*) Tamara with her parents *c.*1944 – T.A.

Page 57 Crowds waiting to see the embalmed body of Stalin, lying in state in Moscow, March 1953. © R.I.A. Novosti Image Gallery – 179810711 – Stalin's Funeral.

Page 63 Tamara about 1956 – T.A.

Page 71 Tamara and Slava's wedding on 26th April 1959 – T.A.

Page 81 Tamara, her son Sergei and her mother in the 1960s when she was working for Georgi Fedyashin at APN Novosti - T.A.

Page 89 Tamara and her son later in the 1960s – T.A.

Page 120 (*Top*) Tamara and Norman Swallow outside Mosfilm sound studio in summer of 1967 – T.A./M.D.

Page 120 (*Bottom left*). Michael Darlow with Tamara and Intourist interpreter Natasha outside the Kremlin in Moscow – T.A./M.D.

Page 120 (*Bottom right*). Norman Swallow, Russian cameraman Yuri Spilny and Michael Darlow filming *Ten Days That Shook the World* – T.A./M.D.

Page 121 (*Top left*) Lyuba Orlova, who had been Stalin's favourite film star, and Norman Swallow at the end of a long dinner in the Alexandrov's Moscow flat. © Grigori Alexandrov, deceased no known heirs.

Page 121 (*Top right*) Michael Darlow and Norman Swallow in front of statue of Lenin in the Museum of the Revolution in Moscow – T.A./M.D.

Page 121 (*Middle left*) *Ten Days That Shook the World* composer Revol Bunin, his wife Michael Darlow, Norman Swallow and Tamara. © Grigori Alexandrov, deceased no known heirs.

Page 121 (*Bottom*) Tamara, Michael Darlow, Georgi Bolshakov, Ludmila Borozdina, Lyuba Orlova and Norman Swallow in the Alexandrov's dacha outside Moscow. © Grigori Alexandrov, deceased no known heirs.

Page 127 (*Top*) Piskariovskoye Memorial, Leningrad (Found on website: http://djgagnon.tumblr.com.post/46458592161/piskariovskoye-memorial.cemtery-four-hundred (copyright not attributed).

Page 127 (*Bottom left*) Piskariovskoye Memorial, Leningrad. Each long low mound contains 8,000 of those who died during the siege of Leningrad in World War II. © TwoTumblrmkcozyn13A lgd3g3go!-1280.

Page 127 (*Bottom right*) Olga Bergholtz, Russian poet who remained in Leningrad throughout the 900 day siege. © Wikimedia Commons – public domain. Taken in 1930.

Page 139 (*Left*) Tamara in about 1969. T.A.

Page 139 (*Right*) Tamara's son Sergei with Tamara's mother in 1976 – T.A.

Page 151 Tamara with Henri Brandt – T.A.